YORK NOTES

# A STREETCAR NAMED DESIRE

## TENNESSEE WILLIAMS

## NOTES BY HANA SAMBROOK

Longman

York Press

YORK PRESS
322 Old Brompton Road, London SW5 9JH

PEARSON EDUCATION LIMITED
Edinburgh Gate, Harlow,
Essex CM20 2JE, United Kingdom
Associated companies, branches and representatives throughout the world

© Librairie du Liban Publishers 1998, 2003

First published 1998
This new and fully revised edition first published 2003
15  14  13  12  11  10

ISBN: 978-0-582-78424-6

Designed by Michelle Cannatella
Typeset by Land & Unwin (Data Sciences), Bugbrooke, Northamptonshire
Produced by Pearson Education Asia Limited, Hong Kong

# CONTENTS

## PART FOUR
### CRITICAL HISTORY

## PART FIVE
### BACKGROUND

## PART ONE

## INTRODUCTION

## HOW TO STUDY A PLAY

Studying on your own requires self-discipline and a carefully thought-out work plan in order to be effective.

- Drama is a special kind of writing (the technical term is '**genre**') because it needs a performance in the theatre to arrive at a full interpretation of its meaning. Try to imagine that you are a member of the audience when reading the play. Think about how it could be presented on the stage, not just about the words on the page.

- Drama is always about conflict of some sort (which may be below the surface). Identify the conflicts in the play and you will be close to identifying the large ideas or themes which bind all the parts together.

- Make careful notes on themes, character, plot and any sub-plots of the play.

- Why do you like or dislike the characters in the play? How do your feelings towards them develop and change?

- Playwrights find non-realistic ways of allowing an audience to see into the minds and motives of their characters, for example , aside or music. Consider how such dramatic devices are used in the play you are studying.

- Think of the playwright writing the play. Why were these particular arrangements of events, characters and speeches chosen?

- Cite exact sources for all quotations, whether from the text itself or from critical commentaries. Wherever possible find your own examples from the play to back up your opinions.

- Where appropriate, comment in detail on the language of the passage you have quoted.

- Always express your ideas in your own words.

These York Notes offer an introduction to *A Streetcar Named Desire* and cannot substitute for close reading of the text and the study of secondary sources.

 **QUESTION**

How many conflicts can you identify in *A Streetcar Named Desire*?

## READING *A STREETCAR NAMED DESIRE*

Reading the text of a play as a piece of literary work will always raise the question: to what extent is a play written to be read instead of being performed on the stage?

**QUESTION**

What are the advantages of *reading* a play?

With the exception of some plays mentioned below, the reader must assume that it has been written to be acted on the stage before an audience, in an appropriate setting. Unlike the audience in a theatre, the readers are free to use their imagination, almost to participate in the creation of a performance. There is a good deal of satisfaction in doing this. On a more practical level, the readers can go back and reread a scene that has caught their imagination or has presented a problem of interpretation.

Again on a practical level, there need be no break in their reading (no interval for the sale of ice-cream!), and they can give full weight to the significance of the author's use of the conventional division of a play into Acts and scenes. Thus Tennessee Williams divides *A Streetcar Named Desire* into eleven short scenes, not acts (see **Structure** in **Dramatic techniques** on this peculiarity of the play). Though an audience in a theatre will know that Williams has divided his play into eleven short scenes instead of the conventional three acts (the break between the scenes usually indicated by the dimming of the stage), the speed of the action on the stage will not allow them to pause to consider the playwright's possible reason for doing this. Indeed the audience will be carried along by the drama before them, and will have neither the leisure nor the inclination to analyse the structure of the play.

Another advantage of reading a play is of course its ready availability in book form. Years may pass before a piece of theatre can be seen on the stage (see **Critical history**). By contrast the readers of a play are free to see it in their minds any time they choose. With paperback editions easily obtainable they can read and analyse the play at leisure.

Nevertheless, readers should always bear in mind that, like most plays, *A Streetcar* was written for the stage, and that Williams expected his play to be seen and *heard* (just as important: the readers of a play will not hear a different variety of voices in their heads). The private performance in the reader's mind will be hazy, with shadowy figures speaking in one kind of voice; but the one undoubted advantage of this approach is that the full value of the words as literature will be realised and appreciated.

Of course, there have been plays written expressly to be read, which the author never intended for the stage. Labelled **closet drama**, such plays include John Milton's *Samson Agonistes* (1671), Percy Bysshe Shelley's *Prometheus Unbound* (1820) and *The Cenci* (1819), William Wordsworth's *The Borderers* (1842), and, in the twentieth century, Dylan Thomas's *The Doctor and the Devils* (1953), the scenario for a film (never to be made) about the Edinburgh body-snatchers. This last perhaps falls outside the definition of closet drama as it was intended to be read as a film, not a play.

Certainly, there have been stage performances of such plays (some years ago *Samson Agonistes* was staged during the Edinburgh Festival), but the author's intention is clearly stated in the Preface: 'Division into Act and Scene, referring chiefly to the stage (to which this work was never intended) is here omitted'.

Closet drama has never been a preferred medium. Rarely chosen as a genre by a playwright, rarely acclaimed by its readers, it must be seen as a strong argument in favour of a play written for the stage, acted to be seen and heard by an audience willing to lose itself in the spectacle before it.

Tennessee Williams certainly wrote his plays for the stage and was eager to see them performed. Yet his stage directions (of which the theatre audience would remain unaware) often go far beyond practical instructions and can only be fully appreciated when reading the play. Thus in the description of Elysian Fields at the start of Scene 1, Williams speaks of the evening sky that '*gracefully attenuates the atmosphere of decay*'. When Blanche Dubois arrives on the scene, the description of her unsuitably dainty dress ends with the ominous words '*There is something about her uncertain*

**QUESTION**

A characteristic of closet drama is its static quality. Can you imagine *A Streetcar* with all the actors standing still and reciting their lines?

**CHECK THE BOOK**

Even a cursory glance through *Samson Agonistes* will enable you to identify the marks of a true closet drama: the action is described by a chorus and is not seen on the stage, and there are no directions for stage setting.

**CONTEXT**

An earlier version of the play was entitled 'The Moth'.

**CHECK THE BOOK**

The sexual tension between Blanche and Stanley, heightened by class differences, may bring to mind D. H. Lawrence's Lady Chatterley and the gamekeeper Mellors in the 1928 novel *Lady Chatterley's Lover,* or August Strindberg's Miss Julie and the footman Jean in the play *Miss Julie* (1888). Such parallels serve to underline the play's violent and tragic ending.

*manner ... that suggests a moth'* (p. 5), words that hint at her fragility and her helplessness, and foreshadow her tragic end. Yet the beauty of the language should not distract us from its meaning: the metaphors are a very accurate directive for the actors and the staging.

Did Tennessee Williams expect his plays to be read? Was that why he paid as much attention to the wording of the stage directions as to the words spoken by the characters in the play? Or is it simply that a writer like Williams found metaphors the most accurate means of conveying what he expected to see on the stage? If you are reading the play and trying to envisage a stage performance of it, Williams' stage directions are a twofold bonus for you: they help you to imagine the setting, certainly; but in addition they offer you the pleasure of reading them, a pleasure that cannot be shared by theatre audiences. The use of language in *A Streetcar Named Desire* will be discussed later (see **Language and style**), yet it is useful for the readers to be aware of some aspects of it when starting to read this play.

A stage performance will, to some extent, blot out the characters the readers have created in their imagination. Anyone who has seen Vivien Leigh and Marlon Brando as Blanche and Stanley in the 1951 film version of *A Streetcar Named Desire* will find their powerful screen presences difficult to dismiss. Again, reading the play offers advantages here. With no actors' faces and voices to impose themselves on the reader's imagination, there is naturally more freedom of interpretation. The faces and voices lack definition but they lend themselves all the more to the reader's imagination.

When reading a play we become more fully aware of its literary aspects. On the stage the words spoken by the actors serve to create tension, to move the action forward, and as spectators all we are aware of is how convincing and compelling the actors' words are. During our reading of the play we can appreciate the beauty of the language as much as its dramatic effectiveness. We also have time to think of parallels and echoes, which will add to our understanding of the play. Not only aware of the clashes of character, we have time to realise the underlying causes perhaps more clearly than the theatre audiences, though we do not necessarily respond to the play with deeper emotion.

When reading the play we can also consider its autobiographical element. Tennessee Williams himself was aware of the importance of this. He said: 'I must find characters who correspond to my own tensions' (quoted in *Tennessee Williams: Rebellious Puritan* by Nancy Tischler, p. 246). *A Streetcar Named Desire* is not so closely based on Tennessee Williams' own experiences as his *The Glass Menagerie*, but there are aspects of the play that reflect his own story. A man who had been nicknamed Tennessee (see **Background** on **Tennessee Williams**) was certainly as aware of his Southern-ness as his Blanche was. Blanche's betrayal by her own sister which results in her committal to a mental hospital is a parallel of Tennessee Williams' own guilt-ridden feelings about his sister Rose who was lobotomised during his absence at university, and sent to a state mental hospital. Such considerations do not, of course, add to our appreciation of the play, but they do deepen our understanding of it.

Finally, reading about Blanche's promiscuity, hinted at by her flirtatious manner and cruelly exposed by Stanley, we may well remember Tennessee Williams' own homosexual liaisons. It has been suggested that, in creating Blanche, Tennessee Williams was indulging in imaginative cross-dressing, that he wrote of a promiscuous heterosexual woman because homosexuality was then still illegal in most American states. However we view this possibility, we can appreciate that the title of the play, *A Streetcar Named Desire*, conveys Tennessee Williams' view of any sexual passion as an inexorable force that will take its victim along a path to self-destruction that is as unbending as the tracks of a streetcar. Again, his view of sexual passion as a force taking its victim to self-destruction may contribute to our understanding of Williams' attitude to his homosexuality (see **Background** on **Tennessee Williams**).

**QUESTION**

The streetcar is referred to only twice in the play. How does the title nonetheless dominate our perception of the play?

Obviously such speculations are not possible for the audience in a theatre, carried along by the speed of the action and by their own immediate reactions. When thinking and talking about the performance later, the spectators will touch fleetingly on topics that come to mind during the reading of a play. Here the reader of the play is in a position of advantage, able to go back and review an earlier scene in the light of later events. It is arguable of course that

**CONTEXT**

Elia Kazan, who directed the film version of *A Streetcar*, remarked of Williams: 'Everything in his life is in his plays, and everything in his plays is in his life'.

speculation about the autobiographical aspects of a play or its literary antecedents is in the last resort irrelevant: the play's the thing.

Yet any thoughts that increase our interest in the play and widen our perception of it are valuable and enriching. It is hoped that these Notes will stimulate the readers' interest in the play by encouraging them to consider the questions it raises.

The first reading of *A Streetcar Named Desire* should be for the pleasure of discovering what the play is about. When rereading the play, the students should move beyond the simple storyline to a more critical approach. The questions touched on here, as well as other aspects of the play, will be discussed in the following pages.

## PART TWO

# THE TEXT

## NOTE ON THE TEXT

Tennessee Williams started work on *A Streetcar Named Desire* in 1945. Early in the year he wrote the first version, entitled 'The Moth' (evidently the metaphor of Blanche as a delicate, doomed moth caught his imagination quite early on). He then put the play aside, returning to it a little later in the same year.

He named this second version 'Blanche's Chair in the Moon' from an image in his mind of a young woman sitting in a chair in the moonlight, waiting for a lover who never comes. Blanche took centre stage again. By the summer of 1945 the play was given another title again, 'The Poker Night'. As the title implies, the play no longer centred on Blanche alone. The poker players of Scenes 3 and 11 of the final version of the play now take up their places, their comments on the game providing a counterpoint to Blanche's fantasies. In the final version she is unquestionably the central figure, and the card players' gesture of courtesy in the last scene (in contrast to their behaviour in Scene 3) makes it clear that Blanche has achieved tragic status.

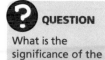

**QUESTION**

What is the significance of the changes in the title of the play?

The changes in the title indicate a shift of emphasis in the play, but there were other changes as well. To begin with, the family at the centre of the play was Italian, but later the brother-in-law became an Irishman and the two sisters turned into Southern belles. The change is significant, given that since its defeat in the American Civil War, the South's image had been that of a nation mourning for a lost way of life. The two sisters' contrasting choices of lifestyles – Stella's happy marriage to a man from a lower class, who satisfies her sexually, and her sister's miserable promiscuity against the background of disintegrating Southern grandeur – encapsulate the alternatives facing the South and point to the tragic end of the play.

Later again, the brother-in-law became a Polish-American. Most of the Polish immigrants before the 1940s and 1950s were not political refugees, or middle class – they were labourers, mostly uneducated, who were looked down upon. The change was made to emphasise the class element in the play, which adds another dimension to the sexual tension between Blanche and Stanley.

The play was first published in New York by New Directions in 1947. It was reissued, with an introduction by Tennessee Williams, by New American Library, New York, in 1951. By this time the play had been successfully staged in New York. The Dramatists' Play Service, New York, published an acting edition in 1953.

In Britain *A Streetcar Named Desire* was first published in London in 1949 by John Lehmann, and reissued in 1956 by Secker & Warburg, London, in a collection entitled *Four Plays*. A paperback edition in one volume with *The Glass Menagerie* appeared under the Penguin imprint in 1959 in their Penguin Plays series. A volume entitled *A Streetcar Named Desire and Other Plays* (containing *A Streetcar Named Desire*, *Sweet Bird of Youth* and *The Glass Menagerie*) was published in the Penguin Twentieth-Century Classics in 1962 and reissued in Penguin Classics in 2000.

In 1984 a Methuen Student Edition of the play was published, with notes by Patricia Hern, and with stills from the 1951 film version of the play. This edition was used in the preparation of these Notes.

Readers might also be interested in the stage history of *A Streetcar Named Desire*. It was first performed in the United States in November 1947 in Boston under the direction of Elia Kazan, and in December of the same year in New York. Jessica Tandy played Blanche and Marlon Brando took the part of Stanley. Later Blanche was played in turn by Uta Hagen and Tallulah Bankhead (herself a Southerner from Alabama) while Brando was replaced for a time by Anthony Quinn. The British premiere was in 1949 at the Aldwych Theatre in London under the direction of Laurence Olivier.

**CHECK THE FILM**

If you are unable to see the play on stage, watch the 1951 film version of the play, directed by Elia Kazan. Vivien Leigh and Marlon Brando played the leading parts to considerable acclaim. Significantly, there has never been a remake of Kazan's film, seen perhaps as the definitive version.

# SYNOPSIS

The play opens on a May evening outside a shabby house in a rundown street in New Orleans, grandly named Elysian Fields. The house belongs to Eunice and Steve Hubbel, and Stanley and Stella Kowalski rent an apartment there.

Eunice is sitting on the steps of the house with a black neighbour when an incongruously dainty woman comes round the corner, carrying a suitcase. She is Stella Kowalski's older sister, Blanche Dubois, arriving on a visit. She accepts Eunice's invitation to wait for Stella in the Kowalskis' apartment.

Stella returns and though the sisters embrace affectionately, an underlying tension makes itself felt. Blanche seems on the defensive, having sold the family property, Belle Reve. The circumstances of the sale are never fully explained.

When Stanley returns home he accepts Blanche's presence quite amiably, but it soon becomes obvious that her genteel pretensions will clash with his macho self-confidence. Through his questioning of Blanche we learn that she had been married and that her husband is dead.

The next evening (Scene 2) Stanley's friends Mitch, Steve and Pablo are coming to play poker, and Stella decides to take her sister out for the evening. Stanley resents the arrangement and, when Stella tells him of the loss of Belle Reve, he suspects that Stella, and he with her, has been cheated by her sister out of her rightful share of the sale.

He pulls out Blanche's large trunk and accusingly displays all her finery as her spoils of the sale. When Blanche comes in after her bath, she flirts with him, but her flirtatious, playful manner arouses his suspicions in another way. Though uneducated, he is no fool, and he realises that his sister-in-law is behaving like a streetwalker. He demands to see the legal papers concerning the sale, explaining that Stella is pregnant which makes him all the more anxious about his rights.

**CONTEXT**

'Belle Reve', the name of the Dubois family mansion, means 'beautiful dream' in Creole French.

 **CHECK THE NET**

Stanley believes that Louisiana (a former French colony) follows the Code Napoléon, the French legal code. But the Codes of Louisiana were not simple adaptations; search for 'Code Napoléon and Louisiana' to learn more.

Much later the same evening (Scene 3) when the sisters return from their evening out, the poker game is still in progress. Stanley has been drinking and he resents Blanche's interest in one of the players, the shy Mitch, a bachelor.

There is a violent scene, and Stanley hits his wife. The hysterical Blanche takes her sister up to Eunice's flat, but later she is shocked to find that Stella has gone back to her husband and is in bed with him.

**CONTEXT**

Notice that Williams makes use of a conventional theatrical device, that of the unseen eavesdropper.

The next day (Scene 4) Stella makes it clear to her sister that she loves her husband and has no intention of leaving him in spite of his brutality. Stanley overhears Blanche's condemnation of him.

Spurred on by his resentment of Blanche (Scene 5) Stanley makes enquiries about her and discovers that she was forced to leave Laurel, her home town, because of her reckless promiscuity. His hints about her past terrify Blanche, and she tries to explain to her sister her past behaviour and her terror of growing old. She admits that she is hoping to marry Mitch, and Stella encourages her hopes. Waiting for Mitch, Blanche flirts recklessly with a young subscription collector.

Blanche's evening out with Mitch is not a success (Scene 6). Mitch is painfully aware of his dullness. He comes in for a nightcap, and to begin with they converse awkwardly. Gradually they begin to talk more seriously, Mitch about his ailing mother and Blanche about her husband's suicide after she found him in bed with another man. Moved by her tragic story, Mitch takes her in his arms.

It is now September (Scene 7), and it is Blanche's birthday. A birthday dinner is planned, to which Mitch has been invited. Stella is decorating the birthday cake when Stanley comes in triumphantly with full details of Blanche's scandalous past. Stella refuses to believe all the stories about her sister and is appalled to learn that Stanley has told Mitch everything. Blanche emerges from the bathroom in high spirits, but she soon senses that something is wrong.

Less than an hour later (Scene 8) the dismal dinner is over. Blanche tries in vain to ring Mitch and is growing more and more frightened.

Stanley has a birthday present for her – a bus ticket back to Laurel. Stella reproaches him for his cruelty, but stops abruptly. Her labour pains have started.

Left alone in the apartment (Scene 9) Blanche has been drinking. Mitch arrives, unshaven and a little drunk. Blanche is overwhelmed to see him, but soon realises that his attitude towards her has changed. He accuses her of having lied to him about her age and about her past. While admitting what she had done Blanche tries to explain the reasons for her behaviour. Mitch has no desire to understand her, and to show his contempt for her he tries to rape her. Her wild cries frighten him and he runs off.

Alone once more (Scene 10), Blanche goes on drinking steadily. Befuddled by drink and confused by her own fantasies, she dresses up in her tawdry finery while trying to pack her trunk.

Stanley arrives, a little drunk, having been sent home by the hospital, as the baby is not expected to arrive before morning. He mocks Blanche's fabrications about a cruise with a rich admirer and about Mitch's penitent return. There is tension between them and Blanche is frightened. Her terror arouses Stanley and he carries her off to the bedroom to rape her.

Some weeks pass (Scene 11) and once more Stanley and his friends are playing poker. Except for Stanley none of the men has much heart for the game. Blanche is heard offstage, having a bath, while Stella is busy packing her sister's trunk. Eunice comes in and from her conversation with Stella we learn that Stella has arranged for her sister to be taken away. Stella explains that she cannot believe Blanche's story and go on living with her husband. Blanche believes that she is going on holiday with her old admirer.

> **CONTEXT**
>
> The repetition of the poker party under very different circumstances heightens the tension.

A doctor and a matron from a mental hospital arrive. Blanche is frightened and tries to run away, but the matron grabs her and holds her. The doctor's calm, courteous manner calms her and she leaves on his arm. The sobbing Stella is given her child to hold and, soothed by Stanley's caresses, she yields to his lovemaking.

# THE TEXT

**GLOSSARY**

**L & N tracks** the tracks of the Louisiana & Nashville railroad

**Polacks** contemptuous American term for people of Polish origin

**is Mass out yet** a coarse joke depending on the similarity of pronunciation between 'Mass' and 'my ass'

## SCENE 1

- Blanche arrives in Elysian Fields.
- There is an undercurrent of tension in the meeting between Blanche and Stella. Blanche admits the loss of Belle Reve.
- There is an uneasy meeting between Blanche and Stanley.

On a May evening in a rundown quarter of New Orleans, in a street ironically named the Elysian Fields, two women, one white and one black, are sitting on the steps of the shabby corner house, enjoying the evening air. The white woman is Eunice who, with her husband Steve, owns the house. Stanley and Stella Kowalski rent an apartment there.

Two men come round the corner – Stanley Kowalski and his friend Mitch. Stanley bellows to his wife that he is on his way to the bowling alley. Stella promises to follow.

As the men leave, a daintily dressed woman appears, carrying a suitcase. She is Blanche Dubois, Stella's elder sister, arriving on a visit. Eunice invites Blanche to wait in the Kowalskis' apartment while the black neighbour fetches Stella. When Stella arrives, the sisters embrace but underlying tensions soon make themselves felt.

Stanley comes in and greets Blanche amicably enough. An uneasy conversation follows, dominated by Stanley's self-assurance. Blanche tells him about the death of her husband some years ago.

**CONTEXT**

The words 'suggests a moth' hint at Blanche's fragility; we may remember that an earlier version of the play was entitled 'The Moth'.

## COMMENTARY

The first scene introduces several themes that will dominate the play. Quite early on we are made aware of Blanche's craving for drink. We also realise that her drinking does not go unnoticed either by her sister or by her brother-in-law – his remark 'Liquor goes fast in hot weather' (p. 14) indicates this. In a play the point is stressed by repetitive action while in a novel it might be made by the **authorial voice**.

Also manifest is Blanche's awareness of social distinctions, which shows itself in the offhand manner in which she accepts both Eunice's and her neighbour's acts of kindness. To Blanche these are services naturally expected of her social inferiors. Her attitude towards these two women prepares us for her condemnation of Stella's way of life, and, implicitly, of her husband.

Another aspect of her character revealed in this scene is her vanity and her need of flattery. There is **pathos** in this: Blanche is afraid of growing old and losing her looks, and needs flattery to banish her terrors. Appealing in her vulnerability she is nevertheless very much the older sister, treating Stella as a child and expecting her to run errands.

Our attention is drawn immediately to Blanche – the greater part of the scene is devoted to building up her character by showing her actions and her reactions to the other characters (see **Focus** in **Dramatic techniques**).

Stanley of course also makes an impact: though we do not see much of him in this scene, Tennessee Williams sketches a portrait of him in stage directions that stress the sexual magnetism of this '*gaudy seed-bearer*' (p. 14), explaining Stella's infatuation. This sketch of Stanley's personality is, of course, withheld from the audience, who will rely on the actor to convey the full force of Stanley's personality.

But what of Stella herself? How much do we learn about her beyond what we learn from her words and actions? Her part in the play is by no means insignificant, yet the introductory stage directions offer no description beyond '*a gentle young woman*' (p. 4). The spectators will see the actress on the stage but the readers of the play must use their imagination and start to piece together a picture of Stella.

Two themes introduced in Scene 1 cannot be fully appreciated by those who read the play rather than attending a performance. The '*blue piano*' and the '*polka*' are heard now, and will be heard

> **CONTEXT**
>
> In classical mythology Elysian Fields are the equivalent of paradise. There is obvious irony in the choice of this name for a rundown street, but we should also remember that the Elysian Fields were the dwelling-place of the dead. Blanche's ultimate fate will be the living death of the asylum.

repeatedly throughout the play. In the stage directions, Williams tells us that the blue piano symbolises this part of New Orleans, but its use as a dramatic device is not consistent. By contrast, the second motif, the polka that Blanche alone can hear (as well as the theatre audience, of course) has considerable dramatic weight; it recalls the last time she danced with her husband, moments before his suicide. The use of a musical motif to alert the audience to a significant fact (here the suicide of Blanche's husband and her guilty feelings about it) is unusual, particularly as it is used not only to create an atmosphere (as the blue piano does to some extent) but also to stress an important aspect of the plot and of Blanche's character. The stage directions offer no explanation, and both the audience and the reader will come to realise the significance of the polka only gradually, the whole story being told in Scene 6. The readers have only Williams' descriptions of the music to guide them, yet perhaps the presence of stage directions stresses its importance more. The audience in a theatre, concentrating on the action, may not pay much attention to background music. After all, we are all used to music in films, and have perhaps learnt to disregard it, though it may still affect our feelings about what we are watching.

**QUESTION**

Those reading the play cannot hear the music. Is their attention drawn to it effectively through the stage directions?

There is another way in which the readers benefit from the stage directions. Tennessee Williams' directions are evocative, precise in their use of imagery, and inevitably stand in contrast to the language used by most of the characters on the stage, with the exception of Blanche and Stella. They serve to underline the uneducated speech of most of the people on the stage. By contrast, Blanche's quotation from Edgar Allan Poe's poem 'Ulalume' reminds us that she is a teacher of English and hints at her cultured background.

The stage directions also draw our attention to the two main characters of the play. Compare the description of Blanche, unsuitably dressed as for a garden party, her white suit in some soft material and her fluttering manner suggesting a moth, and the description of Stanley as a '*gaudy seed-bearer*', proudly aware of his masculinity. Again the stage directions offer help to the reader as much as to the director and cast.

For a more detailed analysis of part of this scene, see **Text 1** in **Extended commentaries**.

## SCENE 2

- The sisters prepare for an evening out.
- Stanley is furious at the loss of Belle Reve.
- Blanche flirts with Stanley and learns that Stella is pregnant.

The following evening, Blanche and Stella are getting ready for an evening out while Stanley is playing poker with his friends. He is clearly annoyed at being left behind. When Stella tells him that Belle Reve is lost, he wants to know how the house was disposed of. He believes that under Louisiana law any property belonging to his wife also belongs to him and he believes that he has been robbed. He betrays here an ignorant man's profound suspicion of other, better-educated people. Furious, he pulls open Blanche's large trunk and displays all her finery, which he believes to be genuine, costly items bought with money that should have been his. Stella is angry and rushes out.

At this point Blanche comes in, radiant after a long bath. While getting ready she flirts with Stanley, but he refuses to pay her the compliments she expects. He demands to see the papers relating to the sale of Belle Reve, and pulls open her trunk to look for them. To Blanche's distress he finds the letters from her dead husband. On being presented with a strongbox of papers he seems a little ashamed and explains that any inheritance would be important because Stella is expecting a baby.

Stella comes in and the sisters embrace. As they set out, Stanley's friends arrive.

### COMMENTARY

In this scene Stanley's antagonism to Blanche grows, as do his suspicions about her. Both the motive and the means for her destruction are now becoming clear, as the playwright prepares the ground for the inevitable calamity.

Stanley's hostility is rooted in his sharp awareness of the class differences between himself and Blanche (and by implication his wife as well), and his instinctive reaction is to pull her down to his level. The sexual implications are obvious: his sexuality is his means of domination. Later on, in Scene 8, he says this to Stella quite explicitly: 'I pulled you down off them columns [of Belle Reve] and how you loved it' (p. 68).

This class antagonism is intensified by Stanley's suspicions that he has been cheated by the smart-talking Blanche. When he pulls out all Blanche's clothes and jewellery he betrays his ignorance of the true value of the articles. Again he is at a loss and his resentment grows because his wife mocks him.

Williams has divided the scene into two parts: first we have Stella instructing her husband how to treat the highly-strung visitor, and telling him of the loss of Belle Reve. Already resentful, Stanley explodes in anger at being swindled, and grows angrier still when his wife laughs at him for overestimating the value of Blanche's wardrobe.

**CONTEXT**

Blanche, in her red robe, is posturing flirtatiously; surely there is a suggestion here of the scarlet woman of the Bible (Revelation 17). This signal may be picked up more easily on the printed page.

When Stella rushes off angrily, the second part of the scene begins with Blanche making an appearance in her red robe. Blind to Stanley's rage she postures flirtatiously. Her manner is such that it arouses Stanley's suspicions in another direction. He is experienced and shrewd enough to sense that his sister-in-law's provocative behaviour is more fitting for a prostitute than for a schoolteacher. He now begins to wonder about her past: 'If I didn't know that you was my wife's sister I'd get ideas about you!' (p. 21).

This then might be seen as the main function of the scene – to set the tragedy in motion. The warning signals would be picked up easily by the audience in the theatre, especially in the second half, with Stanley's smouldering rage set against Blanche's misguided playfulness. The readers of the play are guided by Williams' stage directions and the printed text of the dialogues – and their own imagination.

A new motif is introduced in this scene and will recur again and again: Blanche's passion for taking long baths. On a purely practical level, this habit is obviously very irritating to the other occupants of the apartment and will increase the tension significantly. As so often with Tennessee Williams, however, there is a symbolic aspect to this obsessive habit. It is used to symbolise Blanche's yearning for purification from guilt for her husband's death, and for her many sexual peccadilloes. If in the course of the play, the motif strikes us as repetitive and intrusive, it should be remembered that in the continuing action of the play on the stage it will not force itself on the audience's attention to the same extent. By contrast, the blue piano, which can stand for the spirit of the French quarter of New Orleans or more generally for vitality and pleasure, can also signal a change to a lower key in the mood of the scene. Providing a musical background with no specific message, it remains neutral: '*the perpetual "blue piano"*'.

There are ambiguities in this scene: why is Blanche frightened by the tamale vendor's cry 'Red hots! Red hots!' (p. 23)? And what does she mean by the reference to the Gospels, 'The blind are – leading the blind!' (p. 24)? In the theatre, in a menacing atmosphere created by the first conflict between Blanche and Stanley, the audience will accept Blanche's despairing cry unquestioningly. When reading the play, while unable to arrive at a clear interpretation of the last part of this scene, we still identify Blanche's terror and can accept the approach of a catastrophe.

> **CONTEXT**
>
> In Matthew 15:14, Jesus says 'And if the blind lead the blind, both shall fall into a ditch'. The implication of the proverb here seems to be one of impending disaster.

## SCENE 3

- The sisters return.
- The poker game is still on.
- Stanley is drunk and resentful of Mitch's interest in Blanche.
- A violent row erupts and Stanley hits Stella.
- Stella is taken to Eunice's apartment by the hysterical Blanche, but returns to her husband.
- Blanche is shocked; Mitch comforts her.

> **GLOSSARY**
>
> **One-eyed jacks** knaves of spades and hearts
>
> **wild** having a value to be decided on by the players
>
> **Ante up!** Let's play for higher stakes!
>
> **Openers** opening bids

Much later that night the men are still playing poker. The sisters return and Stanley snubs Blanche for her genteel airs. She shows interest in the shy Mitch, especially noting that he is not married.

As the sisters talk, Stanley orders them to be quiet and turns off Blanche's radio. She turns it on again and Stanley throws it out of the window. Stella rushes at him, and he hits her.

His friends hold him, speaking gently to him, but Blanche runs in hysterically to collect Stella's clothes. Both sisters go upstairs, intending to sleep in Eunice's apartment.

Stanley sobers up and shouts for his wife. Stella appears and they embrace passionately. Blanche is appalled to find that her sister has gone back to her husband. Mitch comforts her, explaining that the Kowalskis are 'crazy about each other' (p. 34). His soft voice calms Blanche, and they sit on the steps talking.

## COMMENTARY

In this scene the relations between the main characters are clarified further. The stage directions deserve our attention for the vivid description of the poker game, especially Williams' reference to a Van Gogh painting of a similar scene. It underlines the significance of the visual elements, of light and of hard primary colours, in this scene, linking them to the harsh masculinity of the men.

The dramatic purpose of the poker party is to demonstrate Stanley's domination over his friends through the way in which he makes all the decisions about the game. The scene shows their devotion to him through their tender handling of him when he is drunk.

Particularly important for the plot is the relationship between Mitch and Stanley. That the latter is jealous of Mitch's interest in Blanche is made clear by his calling Mitch back to the poker game and particularly by the fact that he is watching Mitch: 'He was looking through them drapes' (p. 28) – at Blanche. The sequence of cause and effect may be traced also in Stanley's drunken rage when he hits Stella. That she returns to him that same night is further proof of the strength of her passion, in which his violent behaviour is part of the attraction. Blanche's hysterical determination to take Stella away from her husband (which continues into the next scene) is not forgotten or forgiven by Stanley, and makes him all the more determined to be rid of the unwelcome visitor. The animosity between the two, with its sexual undertones brought into play by Blanche's flirtatious behaviour, foreshadows the shocking climax that will destroy Blanche's sanity.

In this scene we also learn more about Blanche: her vanity betrays her into the foolish lie about Stella's age, and into the equally foolish claim that she has come in order to help out as her sister has not been well. We also notice curious inconsistencies in her behaviour. Blanche's seductive posturing, half-undressed in the gap between the curtains to the bedroom, will be remembered when Stanley reveals her promiscuous past (Scene 7). To her such behaviour is instinctive when there are men around. Her behaviour underlines the contradictions in her character, the genteel Southern lady who expects men to stand up when she comes in and who cannot bear a rude remark or a vulgar action, and the cheap seductress.

Another light on Blanche's character is thrown by the purchase of a Chinese lantern to put over the light bulb. It will play a part in Mitch's disillusionment with her in Scene 9, but it may also be seen as a symbol of Blanche's refusal to face the ugly reality of her life.

Her conversation with Mitch at the close of the scene emphasises the class differences between them, and draws our attention to the effort he is making to overcome them. The artificiality of Blanche's words stresses her awareness of the cultural gap between them and her desperate determination to attract Mitch. Remember her words 'I need kindness now' (p. 34); moving in their honesty, they will be recalled in the last scene when she says to the doctor: 'I have always depended on the kindness of strangers'. The words are the author's appeal on Blanche's behalf for the audience to understand and pity her.

**QUESTION**

The opening stage directions contrast Stella's sleepy sensuality with her sister's hysteria. Is this an indicator of their relationship in the future?

## SCENE 4

- Blanche appeals to Stella to leave Stanley; Stella refuses.
- Stanley overhears Blanche's condemnation of him.

The following morning Stella is still in bed, alone, peaceful and happy. She is reading '*a book of coloured comics*' (p. 34), a silent reminder that she has joined a world in which comics, not books, are read, that she has accepted her husband's standards and values. Blanche rushes in, hysterical after a sleepless night. She reproaches her sister for going back to her husband and sleeping with him.

Stella explains calmly that Stanley is always violent when drunk and that he is now ashamed of himself. Her calm acceptance outrages Blanche. She wants to leave, taking Stella with her. She listens in disbelief when Stella tells her that she loves her husband and will not leave him.

It is obvious that Stanley's violent behaviour is very much a part of his sexual attraction for his wife. It is equally obvious that Blanche does not see this. She condemns Stanley as a savage, a 'survivor of the stone age' (p. 41), bringing home the raw meat (the reader as well as the theatre audience will recall the blood-stained parcel of meat Stanley throws at his wife in Scene 1). To Blanche Stanley is a brute, and while she tells Stella this, Stanley approaches unseen and hears it all. He withdraws and returns noisily, calling for his wife. They embrace and Stanley grins triumphantly at Blanche over Stella's head.

## COMMENTARY

Though this scene seems at first to provide an interval of calm, the tensions quickly build up. Blanche fails to understand Stella's passionate relationship with her husband. It seems that with all her sexual experience (about which we learn in Scene 7) Blanche has never experienced true passion. When Blanche speaks of the 'rattle-trap street-car' (p. 40) of desire, Stella asks her bluntly whether she has ever ridden in it. Blanche's reply 'It brought me here' can mean simply that the streetcar to Desire brought her to her sister's house, but equally it is a metaphor for the sexual desire that has ruined her life and brought her to New Orleans to live on her sister's charity.

Yet below the surface the sisters do understand one another; they both know that they are speaking of sexual passion. Yet while Stella's passion for her husband endures, Blanche's affairs have been brief, lasting only 'when the devil is in [her]' (p. 40). Stella has no patience with Blanche's hysterical plans, and her irritation shows in her dry ironical comments. She starts to resent her sister's disapproval and harsh criticism of Stanley. Will this play a part in her decision in the last scene?

As well as telling us more about the sisters, the scene also has a dramatic function. Having overheard Blanche's melodramatic condemnation of himself as a brute, an ape-man, Stanley now has even more reason to dislike Blanche and to wish to find a way of getting rid of her. His triumphant grin at the close of the scene promises ill for Blanche.

In spite of its brevity, this scene succeeds in several respects. It illuminates the two sisters' attitudes to passion, stressing the basic difference between them, regardless of common background and the social values they were brought up on. This difference will affect Stella's decision about her sister's fate at the end of the play.

Stanley's overhearing Blanche's condemnation of him (a time-honoured dramatic device) strengthens his dislike of her and gives him good reason to try to get rid of her.

Also, Blanche's hysteria (for instance, in her attempt to telephone her old beau Shep) casts doubt on her sanity. This again is sure to influence Stella's readiness to have her sister committed to a mental hospital.

**CONTEXT**

Tennessee Williams had actually seen in New Orleans a streetcar with the curious destination 'Desire'. Apart from the title of the play, the streetcar is mentioned in Scenes 1 and 4.

## SCENE 5

- Stanley hints at Blanche's past.
- Blanche tries to explain to Stella the reasons for her past behaviour.
- Stella encourages Blanche's hopes of marrying Mitch.
- Blanche flirts with a young man just before Mitch's arrival.

Some time later, a noisy row is heard from the upstairs flat as Eunice accuses Steve of infidelity. She rushes out, with Steve following, while the sisters listen below, amused.

Stanley returns from his bowling, and it is clear from Blanche's nervous behaviour that she is afraid of him, with reason. He tells her that an acquaintance of his remembers meeting her at a disreputable hotel in the town where she taught. Blanche denies this but looks terrified.

Stanley leaves, and Blanche tries to find out how much her sister knows of her past, and to explain the reasons for her past behaviour. She admits that she is nervous: Mitch is coming to take her out, and she is desperate to attract him because she is afraid of growing old and unattractive, and of being alone.

Stella tries to reassure her as she leaves to join Stanley. A young man calls, collecting subscriptions to a paper. Blanche flirts with him, to his embarrassment, and then sends him on his way, just before Mitch's arrival.

**QUESTION**

How does Stanley's refusal to kiss his wife in front of her sister contribute to our understanding of the shocking events of Scene 10?

### COMMENTARY

A threatening undertone runs through this scene. It opens with a violent row between Eunice and Steve, which is followed by a hostile interchange between Stanley and Blanche. It is clear that Stanley has discovered something about Blanche's past and that she is frightened.

In hesitant tones, Blanche talks to Stella about her attempts to gain the protection of men friends. Her description of her efforts to attract and hold men, dressing in the soft colours of butterfly wings, recalls her moth-like first appearance in Elysian Fields. We are reminded of her fragility and vulnerability, and of her justified fears of losing her beauty. She is aware that she is growing older and feels she must prevent men from seeing this. Her use of the metaphor of the paper lantern is a deliberate pointer back to her conversation with Mitch in Scene 3 – 'I can't stand a naked light bulb' (p. 30) – and also forward to Mitch's contemptuous tearing off of the Chinese lantern in Scene 9 (an action repeated by Stanley in Scene 11).

Blanche's confession to Stella about her fears for the future and her hopes of finding safety with Mitch is harrowing because she now admits, however indirectly, her past liaisons and recognises that they were just a way of asserting her existence.

There is a sense of foreboding in this scene as Blanche cries over the stain on her white shirt – is it a symbol of lost innocence or a reminder of her husband's bloody end? We become aware of the inevitability of disaster because we now know that she will always go astray, propelled by sexual greed as well as by an instinctive rejection of the dull security she professes to need. The point is driven home by her flirtation with the young collector for a local newspaper, particularly by what she says to him. The innuendo of 'You make my mouth water' (p. 49) and the open confession of past misdeeds in 'keep my hands off children' (p. 49) tell us quite clearly what was the scandal in Laurel that put an end to Blanche's teaching career and drove her away. The throbbing of the blue music and the distant thunder in the last part of this scene speak perhaps of sexual passion too.

Tennessee Williams uses the brief episode with the young man to show the contradictions in Blanche's character. She is desperate to marry Mitch, yet she is ready to risk her future in this flirtatious episode. Is it an urge to self-destruction? Or is it that she has no real desire for the safety of married life because in her heart she cannot commit herself to a permanent relationship with one man? The moth will flutter and not settle down. Tennessee Williams clearly intends to arouse doubts about Blanche, hence this curious episode, which puts at risk the material and emotional security she desires.

**CONTEXT**

Blanche calls the young man 'my Rosenkavalier!' Literally 'the knight of the rose, Rosenkavalier is the eponymous hero of Strauss's opera (1911).

 **QUESTION**

Do you see the episode with the young subscription collector as an illustration of Blanche's character or as a dramatic device necessary to the plot?

Dramatically this episode does more than make us doubt Blanche's real desires. For most readers – or spectators – there is now no possibility of a happy ending for this wretched woman. The question now remains only when and how the blow will fall.

## SCENE 6

- Blanche's evening out with Mitch has been a failure.
- Back at the apartment Blanche and Mitch talk awkwardly at first.
- They talk more seriously and Mitch suggests marriage.

Well after midnight Mitch and Blanche return. The evening has not been a success, and Mitch feels he has been dull. Blanche invites him in for a nightcap. At first the conversation remains awkward in spite of Blanche's feverish attempts at gaiety. Then they begin to talk more seriously, Mitch of his ailing mother, Blanche of the suicide of her husband after she had found him in bed with another man. Mitch, deeply moved, embraces her as she weeps.

## COMMENTARY

The opening mood of this scene is downbeat and depressing; the evening out has been a failure, and both Mitch and Blanche know it, and are dispirited by their inadequacies.

While Mitch apologises for his dullness, Blanche's reaction is to be feverishly gay, pretending to the incomprehending Mitch that they are in a café on the Left Bank in Paris. Her desperate attempt is of course doomed to failure, and stresses her inability to understand other people, isolated as she is in the world of her imagination.

Her play-acting is a prelude to a dramatic change of mood when she and Mitch talk seriously. It has another purpose as well: to stress her need for make-believe situations which make it possible for her to bear her blighted life. Indeed it might be said that Blanche is almost

**CHECK THE BOOK**

Blanche refers to the novel *La Dame aux Camélias* (1848) by Alexandre Dumas the Younger. Significantly, its heroine is a high-class Parisian call girl. The association is continued with the words '*Voulez-vous coucher avec moi ce soir,*' the standard invitation of a French prostitute.

incapable of facing reality – not only its uglier aspects, but its humdrum ordinary demands as well. She sees Mitch as her salvation, but could she bear the life of the wife of a factory worker?

There are moments in this scene that hint at Blanche's unwillingness to go on with the play-acting inherent in her relationship with Mitch. While pretending to be in a Paris café she bluntly offers to sleep with him, certain that he does not understand French. Again, when speaking to him of her old-fashioned ideas about women's behaviour, she rolls her eyes self-mockingly, knowing that he cannot see her face.

On both these occasions she risks being found out by Mitch. As in the episode with the young man in the preceding scene she recklessly endangers her hard-won position with Mitch, as if in her heart she wished to make sure that for her there never would be the dull safety of marriage. And yet at the close of the scene her humble gratitude is sincere. It puzzles us yet engages our sympathy.

Also worth noting here is the significance of Blanche's incoherent musing about Stanley's dislike of her. Incomprehensible to Mitch, her half-spoken conjecture is that Stanley's dislike of her might be a kind of perverse sexual attraction. Her knowledge of men, gained in all those one-night stands in Laurel, is obvious here though never comprehended by the simple Mitch.

**QUESTION**

Wondering about Stanley's dislike of her, Blanche half defines the sexual tension between them. Are her words clear enough?

As well as casting light on her past, her speculation foreshadows her fatal encounter with Stanley in Scene 10. The rape that will drive her into her fantasy world for good is foretold here and its motive defined accurately, as will be acknowledged by Stanley in the later scene – 'We've had this date with each other from the beginning!' (p. 81).

The dramatic device of forewarning the spectators or readers of what is going to happen is used here only obliquely. It might pass unnoticed in a stage performance of the play, but will be picked up by students of the printed text who have the leisure to give the words their full weight.

The low-key mood of this scene is underlined by the absence of the blue piano. The polka music, on the other hand, plays an important part in Blanche's revelations about her husband's suicide and the reasons for it. The polka has been heard before as an oblique reference to Blanche's past (Scene 1), but only now do we realise its full meaning. In order for the music to be dramatically effective, we must remember that Blanche alone (along with the audience) can hear the polka music and the shot.

## SCENE 7

- Stella is preparing Blanche's birthday dinner.
- Stanley arrives triumphantly with details of Blanche's promiscuous past.
- Mitch has been told and will not be coming.

It is now September, and it is Blanche's birthday. While she is taking a bath, Stella is putting the final touches to the birthday cake. Stanley comes in triumphantly with details of Blanche's scandalous past. She had been promiscuous even while still living at Belle Reve, meeting drunken soldiers at night. When the house was sold she moved to a cheap hotel with a bad reputation, but the management asked her to leave because of her scandalous behaviour. She was dismissed from her teaching post for seducing one of the pupils.

Stella refuses to accept all of this as true, while admitting that Blanche's flighty behaviour had caused concern at home. She blames Blanche's disastrous early marriage and her husband's suicide for it.

She is appalled to learn that Stanley has told Mitch about Blanche's past, thus putting an end to Blanche's hopes of marrying Mitch. When Blanche emerges from the bathroom she realises at once that something has happened and she is frightened.

## COMMENTARY

This is a short scene full of dramatic contrasts. The cheerful mood of pleasant anticipation (Blanche singing in her bath; Stella arranging the birthday table) is shattered when the triumphant Stanley comes in with the full details of Blanche's past. His convincing account of Blanche's shocking behaviour is constantly contrasted with her sentimental song offstage.

The full dramatic impact of the scene relies not on the details of Blanche's past, shocking as they are, but on her ignorance of what is happening outside the bathroom. Stanley's earlier remark, 'It's not my soul I'm worried about!' (p. 61) has not alerted Blanche to the approaching danger. It seems that Stella's criticism of Stanley's behaviour towards Blanche is justified; and that Blanche has become accustomed to his hostility and ignores it. Her bathing, on one level a metaphor for her yearning to be rid of her past (see **Imagery and symbolism**), provides an opportunity in this scene to contrast Stanley's revelations with her ignorance of them. Her blithe singing in the bath, almost within earshot of Stanley's account, plays an important part in raising the tension.

**CONTEXT**

Blanche's playful words, 'Possess your soul in patience!' – a common enough phrase – are an adaptation of the words in St Luke's Gospel (21:19): 'In your patience, possess your souls'.

That Williams planned this is evident in his use of the word 'contrapuntally' in the stage directions. The use of two speakers, one commenting on the other, usually in derogatory terms, is not original; it is employed, for instance, in Shakespeare's *Henry IV, Part II* (1597), Act II Scene 4, where the Prince and Poins listen to Falstaff slandering them to Doll, and make furious comments on what they hear. Williams makes use of a familiar, often used formula to good effect.

## SCENE 8

- The disastrous birthday party is over.
- Stanley gives Blanche a cruel birthday present of a bus ticket back to Laurel.
- A quarrel between Stella and Stanley is interrupted by her labour pains.

**GLOSSARY**

**the Greyhound** a long-distance coach company

*El pan de mais* maize bread without salt (a Mexican folk song)

Less than an hour later Blanche, Stella and Stanley are finishing the dreadful birthday meal, the empty fourth chair reminding us of Mitch's absence. Blanche is making desperate attempts at conversation, but Stanley remains sullen, reacting with fury to his wife's criticism of his table manners. The candle-lighting ceremony fails to lighten the mood, and Stanley's birthday present of a bus ticket back to Laurel shatters Blanche. She rushes off to be sick, and Stella reproaches her husband for his cruelty. Suddenly she stops and asks him to take her to the hospital. Her labour pains have started.

## COMMENTARY

This is a disjointed scene, with changes of mood from embarrassment to violence, to a pathetic attempt at normality, to Stanley's brutality, ending with Stella's abrupt departure for the hospital. For Stella and Stanley the focus now shifts away from Blanche's distress.

Of course, the explanation for his behaviour towards Blanche which Stella has been demanding is now forgotten (and from her words in the last scene of the play will never be asked for); indirectly Stanley has already answered her when he reminds her of their lovemaking, impossible while Blanche is sharing their tiny apartment. Justifying himself, he reminds Stella of the passionate climaxes – 'them coloured lights' (p. 68) – and incidentally throws a light on the nature of their relationship. He brought Stella down from her high social position to his own level, and the humiliation was part of the pleasure for her: ' I pulled you down off them columns and how you loved it'.

**CHECK THE BOOK**

In August Strindberg's play *Miss Julie,* the footman Jean says 'Fall to my level and then I can pick you up again'.

Does Tennessee Williams use the start of Stella's labour as a **deus ex machina** to resolve a difficult situation in the plot? There is certainly an abrupt change of mood, a movement away from Blanche, yet she reclaims our attention in the last moments of the scene. Whether she realises fully her present position or not, she seems different, whispering the repetitive Spanish words in a dazed manner which perhaps foreshadows her descent into unreality.

Of course Stella's labour pains also serve another purpose in the plot. Her departure to the hospital leaves Blanche alone in the apartment for the next two scenes, with tragic results.

In this short scene we sense the mounting tension while the characters on the stage (and the audience) wait for the final blow to fall on Blanche when she is presented with the ticket to Laurel. We may notice, incidentally, that it is not possible to experience the same tense expectation while reading the play; the pauses and silences on the stage are inevitably absent as the reader's eye moves down the page.

The background blue music from the neighbouring bar plays a much less important part in this scene, and fades out altogether in its latter half, making way for the Varsouviana polka. The polka is heard softly when Blanche is presented with her bus ticket, and louder and more insistently at the end of the scene when she emerges from the bathroom into the empty room. In this scene the polka is not so much a reminder of Blanche's dead husband as a general note of disaster.

**CONTEXT**

The very shortness of this scene, with its quick changes of mood, adds to the dramatic tension.

## SCENE 9

- Blanche is alone, drinking.
- Mitch arrives and accuses her of lying about her age and her innocence.
- Blanche tries in vain to explain herself.
- Mitch tries to rape Blanche but her cries frighten him off.

**GLOSSARY**

**boxed out of your mind** insane

*Flores para los muertos* (Spanish) flowers for the dead (there is a strong cult of death in Mexico)

**paddy-wagon** police van, Black Maria

This scene marks a decisive stage in Blanche's disintegration. She is drinking heavily, trying to silence the polka music. Mitch's unexpected arrival revives her hopes at first, but as she chatters feverishly, trying to hide the traces of her drinking, and Mitch refuses to respond to her coquetry, she realises that his attitude has changed. He accuses her of lying – about her age, about her innocence – and tells her what he knows about her past.

At first Blanche responds by trying to explain that her lies are to her the real truth; but realising that Mitch does not understand her meaning at all she tells him the truth he can recognise about her life at Belle Reve. Surrounded by dying old women and 'blood-stained pillow-slips' (p. 74), trying to maintain the pretence of gracious living, she used to slip out at night to meet soldiers from the army camp. Later, after the loss of Belle Reve, she moved to a second-rate hotel to entertain her lovers there. She admits to 'many intimacies with strangers' (p. 73) and the truth, spoken at last, is truly shocking.

Mitch's answer is to try and rape her. His astonishment that a woman like that should object to his advances underlines the total lack of understanding between them, which was obvious earlier in this scene when he ignored Blanche's girlish chatter and her pretence of abstemiousness. Both the audience and the reader grasp now the hopelessness of Blanche's efforts to find contentment with him.

## COMMENTARY

The scene is effective as **melodrama** as Mitch's hostility and Blanche's half-hearted protestations lead up to the violent ending of an attempted rape.

On another level, we witness here, symbolised by the tearing off of the paper lantern (itself an act of violence) the stripping of Blanche's pretensions, which reveals the core of honesty in her thought. She knows that she has been lying, but she knows also that her lies are a truthful attempt to present people with the reality they wish for. Though Mitch is incapable of grasping this, she says 'I didn't lie in my heart' (p. 74), 'I tell what *ought* to be truth' (p. 72). Once Mitch has shown her, by his brutal attempt, that he cannot understand, there remains only one way for her: oblivion through drink.

**QUESTION**

Sound effects (the polka music) and visual effects (the Mexican seller of flowers) are continued here. Which do you find more effective, when envisaging this scene?

In this scene the Varsouviana music is heard repeatedly, and Blanche admits her awareness of it as an insistent reminder of her husband's suicide, always coming to a stop with the sound of a shot. Here the polka stops with Mitch's attempt to rape her, and is replaced after his flight with the melancholy sound of the blue piano.

There is also a visual reminder of death in the figure of the Mexican seller of flowers for the dead, whose cry of '*Flores para los muertos*' (p. 74) accompanies Blanche's harrowing, incoherent description of the deaths at Belle Reve.

This scene also merits attention for the insight it offers into Blanche's character. For the first time we are given some insights into Blanche's behaviour at Laurel. She admits her lies, but she also tells unequivocally the truth about herself. As the next two scenes unfold, we shall see that when her fantasies meet with incomprehension and brutality, she turns for good to her world of make-believe; as Blanche herself says: 'I don't want realism' (p. 72).

For more detailed analysis of part of this scene, see **Text 2** in **Extended commentaries**.

## SCENE 10

- Blanche dresses up, drunk and half crazy.
- Stanley returns home to wait for the baby's birth.
- He laughs at Blanche, mocking her illusions.
- Her terror arouses him and he rapes her.

Blanche has been drinking since Mitch's flight, while trying to pack her belongings. She is dressed in her tawdry finery and talking wildly to herself. Stanley returns from the hospital to await the baby's birth at home. He too has been drinking. Blanche invents a story about a millionaire admirer who has invited her to join him on a cruise, and another story about Mitch returning to beg her forgiveness. Stanley mocks her fantasies, enjoying her distress. Her terror arouses him and he carries her off to the bedroom to rape her.

## COMMENTARY

For Williams this scene was the dramatic climax of the play, with the last scene following as a downbeat **coda**. In Scene 10 he uses every means available to him to create an atmosphere of menace (see **Dramatic techniques** on **Visual and sound effects**).

There is a nightmare quality to this harrowing scene. The opening stage directions, describing Blanche's *'soiled and crumpled'* evening

**GLOSSARY**

**ATO pin** Auxiliary Territorial Officer pin

**Biscayne Boulevard** in Miami

**put on the dog** (US) put on one's best clothes

**a red letter night** a special night, a night to celebrate

**Mardi Gras** a carnival celebrated in New Orleans on Shrove Tuesday, the day before Ash Wednesday when Lent, the period of fasting, begins

**Queen of the Nile** Cleopatra, Queen of Egypt (69–30BC)

**rolled** robbed while drunk

gown and her '*scuffed silver slippers*' at once introduce a sordid note. As she talks of her imaginary admirers, we become aware that her grasp of reality is slipping. When she breaks her mirror angrily after seeing her worn face in it, we remember the old superstition that breaking a mirror brings bad luck. We are warned that a calamity is approaching.

When Stanley returns, half-drunk, there is a moment when he seems to make a friendly gesture towards Blanche, but her instant refusal restores the animosity between them. He does not understand Blanche's biblical allusion 'casting my pearls before swine' (p. 78) and as he takes it as a personal insult, his fury grows.

As Blanche carries on with her fabrications, Stanley turns on her, cruelly destroying all her pretensions. Her terror takes on a visible form as '*grotesque and menacing*' shapes close in around her (p. 79), mirrored by ugly scenes of violence in the street outside the apartment.

Crazy with terror, Blanche tries to telephone for help, but her incoherent message is cut short by Stanley's reappearance in his gaudy wedding-night pyjamas. His use of the phrase 'interfere with you' (p. 80), with its sexual undertones, focuses on what is to follow. Blanche's terror rouses Stanley to take her by force. The inevitability of it, hinted at by their earlier encounters, is here made plain by his last spoken words in this scene: 'We've had this date with each other from the beginning!' (p. 81). In a way, Stanley is right: the tension between them was always sexual to some extent. Blanche was aware of his coarse masculinity, and her provocative behaviour was her response to it.

Williams took considerable risks here by moving away from realism in the stage directions while keeping the dialogue in a realistic key. The question all spectators and readers of this play are bound to ask is whether this scene, so **melodramatic** in its technique, is in fact successful drama. The use of the blue piano is effective in creating a threatening atmosphere, intensified by the deafening roar of the locomotive. The visual representation of evil (briefly repeated in Scene 11) can be impressive in a play that by and large maintains a

**QUESTION**

Is the introduction of menacing shapes and sounds effective, and what does it contribute to the play?

**CHECK THE FILM**

In the film version these shapes are not shown, nor is the discordant music heard. This omission makes for reality, however appalling.

naturalistic presentation through dialogue and action (though not necessarily through the stage directions); but is it effective when used in one single scene?

Readers of the play should remember that on the stage the effect of the *'inhuman voices like cries in a jungle'* (p. 79) and sinuous shadows on the walls round Blanche will be less startling to a theatre audience accustomed to sophisticated stage lighting and sound effects, and ready to accept them as part of the staging. Williams' careful stage directions here indicate that he was anxious to achieve a shocking visual and sound impact in keeping with the shocking spectacle of a man breaking all the taboos and raping his sister-in-law while his wife is giving birth to his child.

This scene is particularly interesting if we are making a comparison between a play on stage and the same play read on the printed page. Are they the same play? To a question of this sort there can never be a single answer, but it is a question worth asking, not least for the light it throws on the nature of theatrical experience as against the readers' participation in the text and the re-creation of it in their minds.

## SCENE 11

- Some weeks later Stella is packing Blanche's belongings.
- A more subdued poker party is in progress.
- Blanche is expecting to be going on a cruise with an admirer but she has been committed to a mental hospital with Stella's approval.
- The doctor and matron from the hospital arrive and Blanche, reassured, leaves on the doctor's arm.
- Stanley comforts Stella by making love to her.

Some weeks have passed. Blanche is taking yet another bath while Stella is packing for her. The men are playing poker again but only Stanley is able to concentrate on the game. We learn that Stella has

**CHECK THE FILM**

In the film version, Stella leaves Stanley at the end, taking the baby with her. This punishment of a rapist was demanded by the Hollywood moral code.

**GLOSSARY**

**drew to an inside straight and made it** took a risk and was successful

**Della Robbia blue** a vivid blue used by the Italian artist Luca della Robbia (c.1400–82) for the background of his reliefs

arranged for her sister to be taken to a mental hospital. Stella explains that, quite simply, if she is to go on living with Stanley she must believe that the story of the rape is the invention of a mentally unstable woman.

Blanche still believes that she is going on a cruise with her old beau Shep. When the hospital doctor and matron arrive she panics and struggles, but is reassured by the doctor's courtesy and leaves on his arm. She ignores her sister, who stands weeping with her baby in her arms. Stella is distressed but Stanley's lovemaking calms her.

## COMMENTARY

This scene, a downbeat **coda** to the **melodrama** of the rape, maintains a subdued mood. The arrangement of the play into eleven short scenes enables the audience to accept the transition from the tragic climax of Scene 10 (which would conclude the traditional third act) to the everyday activities of packing, bathing, card-playing, and discussing clothes and accessories.

At the same time, these actions and conversations by their very similarity to the earlier scenes emphasise the difference. Stella has been crying, and the poker-players (except Stanley) have lost their boisterous good humour. More significantly still, they rise in an act of courtesy when Blanche passes through the room. The paper lantern, which Mitch tore off the light bulb, is torn off again by Stanley and again Blanche cries out as if in physical pain. His action might be seen as a symbolic replay of the rape.

> **CONTEXT**
>
> Stanley asks the other men to remember Salerno. This is a port in southern Italy, the scene of fierce fighting in the Second World War.

Blanche's daydream of a voyage ends in her picturing her death from eating an unwashed grape, and her burial at sea 'in a clean white sack' (p. 85) – again revealing her obsession with cleanliness. The Varsouviana polka is heard through most of the scene, a constant reminder of the early tragedy in Blanche's life. There are visual reminders of the nightmare distortions of Scene 10, as well as echoes of the jungle-like cries, as Stanley's presence brings back the memory of the rape.

While recalling earlier, often melodramatic scenes, the mood here remains subdued, up to the moment of dreadful panic when Blanche abandons her daydream and faces an incomprehensible harsh reality. Like Blanche, the audience is kept in the dark about what is going to happen. Only gradually do we come to understand that Blanche is going to be committed to a mental hospital. The doctor's courtesy calms Blanche and restores the subdued tone of the scene. In this calm atmosphere, Blanche goes out on the doctor's arm, a curiously dignified figure. As she says to him, 'I have always depended on the kindness of strangers' (p. 89), her words recall her thanking Mitch at the end of Scene 3: 'I need kindness now' (p. 34); and we now realise the poignant truth that there has been very little kindness in Blanche's life.

CONTEXT

Blanche's last words in the play are a direct and most effective appeal for the audience's sympathy and pity.

Her quiet dignity is in contrast to her display of vanity and her fussing over her appearance earlier in the same scene. Ancient Greek tragedy demanded for its main theme the downfall of a great person through his/her own pride and arrogance (**hubris**). The opposite is the case here: Blanche Dubois's vanities and moral weaknesses fall away from her in the moment of departure and she achieves the dignity of a tragic heroine. The effect is to diminish the others in the drama: the sobbing, guilt-stricken Stella, begging for reassurance; the blustering, bullying Stanley; the weak, ineffectual Mitch.

In dramatic terms the play ends with a successful **coup de théâtre**. The last scene contains elements of melodrama – Blanche's ignorance of her fate, her panic at hearing Stanley's voice, her struggle with the matron – but the overall effect is muted. The effect of the trivia of Blanche's wardrobe and her costume jewellery is to heighten the dramatic tension. Here again Williams shows the instinct of a dramatist: he creates an ominous quiet to be broken all the more effectively by Blanche's last desperate attempt to escape, and restored again in her dignified departure.

Stanley's lovemaking to Stella provides an ironic coda: she had bartered her sister for sexual gratification, and the bargain is now completed.

For more detailed analysis of part of this scene, see **Text 3** in **Extended commentaries**.

## EXTENDED COMMENTARIES

Above, Williams' play is analysed scene by scene, starting with a summing up of the action, followed by a commentary on the author's handling of the scene. Here by contrast we concentrate on three short extracts from the play, each one just a page or so in length. The commentary will be more detailed, giving due weight to the words and phrases which might not attract special attention in the summary of a whole scene.

In the course of the analysis we should gain insights beyond our appreciation of the verbal skills of the dramatist. The words he uses are, after all, the sole tool of his trade. The actors' speeches, admittedly in Williams' case greatly aided by the stage directions, have to convey the dramatic developments (tell the story, so to speak) and also indirectly to build up the characters whom the actors represent on the stage, and establish the background of the action.

It is clear, then, that the words spoken on the stage (or read in a printed version of the play) are quite uniquely important. As in a poem, each word is chosen with great care, and should be spoken or read with equal care.

## TEXT 1 (SCENE 1, PAGES 12–13)

STELLA: Stop this hysterical outburst and tell me what's happened? What do you mean fought and bled? What kind of –

BLANCHE: I knew you would, Stella. I knew you would take this attitude about it!

STELLA: About – what? – please!

BLANCHE [*slowly*]: The loss – the loss …

STELLA: Belle Reve? Lost, is it? No!

BLANCHE: Yes, Stella.

*They stare at each other across the yellow-checked linoleum of the table.* BLANCHE *slowly nods her head and* STELLA *looks slowly down at her hands folded on the table. The music of the "blue piano" grows louder.* BLANCHE *touches her handkerchief to her forehead.*

**QUESTION**

Do you think that Blanche genuinely does not know why the family estate had to be sold, or is unwilling to admit her part in the disaster?

STELLA: But how did it go? What happened?

BLANCHE [*springing up*]: You're a fine one to ask me how it went!

STELLA: Blanche!

BLANCHE: You're a fine one to sit there *accusing me* of it!

STELLA: *Blanche!*

BLANCHE: I, I, *I* took the blows in my face and my body! All of those deaths! The long parade to the graveyard! Father, mother! Margaret, that dreadful way! So big with it, it couldn't be put in a coffin! But had to be burned like rubbish! You just came home in time for the funerals, Stella. And funerals are pretty compared to deaths. Funerals are quiet, but deaths – not always. Sometimes their breathing is hoarse, and sometimes it rattles, and sometimes they even cry out to you, "Don't let me go!" Even the old, sometimes, say, "Don't let me go." As if you were able to stop them! But funerals are quiet, with pretty flowers. And, oh, what gorgeous boxes they pack them away in! Unless you were there at the bed when they cried out, "Hold me!" you'd never suspect there was the struggle for breath and bleeding. You didn't dream, but I saw! *Saw! Saw!* And now you sit there telling me with your eyes that I let the place go! How in hell do you think all that sickness and dying was paid for? Death is expensive, Miss Stella! And old Cousin Jessie's right after Margaret's, hers! Why, the Grim Reaper had put up his tent on our doorstep! ... Stella. Belle Reve was his headquarters! Honey – that's how it slipped through my fingers! Which of them left us a fortune? Which of them left a cent of insurance even? Only poor Jessie – one hundred to pay for her coffin. That was all, Stella! And I with my pitiful salary at the school. Yes, accuse me! Sit there and stare at me, thinking I let the place go! *I* let the place go? Where were *you*. In bed with your – Polack!

STELLA [*springing*]: Blanche! You be still! That's enough! [*She starts out.*]

BLANCHE: Where are you going?

STELLA: I'm going into the bathroom to wash my face.

BLANCHE: Oh, Stella, Stella, you're crying!

STELLA: Does that surprise you?

> **CONTEXT**
>
> 'I let the place go!' Notice that Stella had never accused her sister of this. Blanche's words, anticipating the reproach she expects, are revealing and self-accusatory.

The first of the three passages, taken from the introductory scene of the play, demonstrates Tennessee Williams' skill in writing dialogue that adds to our understanding of the characters, and also to our store of information about earlier events that have built up the dramatic tensions of the play.

The passage begins during a heated exchange between Stella and Blanche. The two sisters have met, embraced and spoken lightly (and in Blanche's case a trifle condescendingly) about New Orleans, about the Kowalskis' humble apartment, and about Stella's husband. A point has been made about Blanche's nervous state.

Blanche appears ill at ease, and finds it difficult to reveal what she clearly feels she must reveal – the loss of the family mansion, Belle Reve. She expects to be blamed by her sister, and the readers (or spectators) may sense that she does feel guilty and is forestalling any reproaches by her accusations of Stella.

Stella tries to extract the plain facts of the matter from her sister, but Blanche refuses to cooperate. In a long speech, full of unspoken (but strongly hinted at) horrors of her life at Belle Reve she speaks of her own suffering and of her sister's selfish indifference. The speech is accusatory and wounding, and is meant to be: we might remember here the saying that attack is the best defence. The scene ends with Stella in tears, going off to wash her face.

The passage is just one page long, yet we learn a great deal from it. First, the two sisters are quite unlike one another in emotional make-up. Stella interrupts her sister's self-dramatising reproaches with a cutting comment on Blanche's 'hysterical outburst' and on her emotionally loaded phrase 'fought and bled'. Stella quotes Blanche's words deliberately; the repetition is perhaps ironical, intended to lower the emotional temperature and so mock Blanche's histrionics.

Blanche reacts at once by declaring that Stella's attitude was only to be expected. We are made aware that the confrontation follows a long-established pattern of rows between the sisters. Blanche's words 'The loss – the loss ...' show that she still finds it difficult to

**QUESTION**

This brief extract reveals a good deal about the sisters' characters and their relationships. Do we learn as much about Stella as about Blanche?

speak of the loss of the family mansion openly. She is slowly brought to admit that Belle Reve has been sold, and Stella's reaction to the shattering news is as typical of her as Blanche's histrionics are of Blanche. She '*looks slowly down at her hands folded on the table*', her silence eloquent of her distress. Williams pays great attention to detail in his stage directions, right down to the '*yellow-checked linoleum*'. Blanche makes a typically theatrical gesture as she '*touches her handkerchief to her forehead*' – she is reluctant to give any more information.

Stella wants to know the facts, though, and it becomes clear that this is something Blanche cannot, or will not, provide (her confrontation with Stanley in Scene 2 shows this quite clearly). This leaves it open to question whether her inability to give the details is due to her ignorance of business matters, or whether this is deliberate obfuscation of unpleasant and possibly damaging facts. Blanche's words '*accusing me* of it!' are very revealing: as Stella has not spoken a word of reproach, we can only assume that Blanche's own feelings of guilt are prompting her here. Later, in Scene 9, we learn that she already indulged in wild behaviour while still living at Belle Reve, and it may well be that her drinking and her one-night stands contributed to her inability to cope with the sorry financial state of Belle Reve, as much as the expensive funerals.

In Blanche's long speech we notice her use of a metaphor of physical injury – 'I took the blows in my face and my body!'– which echoes her earlier 'I fought and bled'. The images of messy death, of blood and physical pain proliferate in her speech: 'the long parade to the graveyard'; Margaret so swollen with disease that she could not be fitted into a coffin and had to be burned like rubbish; the hoarse breathing, the death rattle of the dying, their desperate clinging to life – 'Don't let me go!'; the bleeding – later, in Scene 9, Blanche tells Mitch of the 'blood-stained pillow-slips' (p. 74).

Blanche's obsession with death is rooted in her appalling experiences at Belle Reve. Her account is all the more affecting for what is left unsaid. We might also notice here the absence of any sentimentality, indeed of any emotional involvement, in her description of the deaths. Is this due to self-discipline, or is it again

> **CONTEXT**
>
> The images of bleeding and death in Blanche's long speech are striking even in the context. We wonder about the image of her husband's violent death here: his memory seems to have conditioned Blanche to retain in her mind the ghostly reality of dying.

her self-absorption and lack of empathy? She may speak jokingly of the 'Grim Reaper' who 'had put up his tent on our doorstep!' but the death scenes she has witnessed are stamped on her mind. Her experiences in her last years at Belle Reve clearly affected her already precarious mental balance. We may remember this later, in Scene 9, when the symbolic figure of the Mexican seller of paper flowers for the dead brings to Blanche's mind 'a house where dying old women remembered their dead men' (p. 74).

Within this dramatic speech we (and Stella) find a few practical comments on the recurrent funeral expenses, not covered by insurance (except for Cousin Jessie's hundred dollars which just paid for her coffin, but not for her funeral). This sudden descent into practicalities is characteristic of Blanche: remember her in Scene 2 when, after her melodramatic outburst at Stanley's desecration of her dead husband's poems, she puts on her glasses to go methodically through a pile of legal documents concerning the mortgaging of Belle Reve.

Blanche's resentment of Stella's absence is obvious. She reminds her sister bitterly that she only came home for the funerals, which are quiet and 'pretty compared to deaths', with 'gorgeous' coffins and beautiful flowers. She reminds Stella of 'my pitiful salary' in an appeal for sympathy, tinged maybe with self-dramatisation. Some of Blanche's resentment is evidently due to sexual jealousy of her younger sister who got away, found a husband and was 'In bed with [her] Polack' while her sister watched over deathbeds. This is a double insult: a hint at Stella's sexual appetite, and the contempt of a Southern aristocrat for a vulgar immigrant.

Though she remains silent while Blanche is attacking her, Stella will not tolerate insults to her husband: 'That's enough!' We may remember here Stella's defence of Stanley in Scene 4. Blanche seems surprised when she realises that Stella is crying. Perhaps this is because Stella is usually firmly in control of herself; however, we may also surmise that self-absorbed as she is, Blanche lacks the insight into other people's feelings.

 **QUESTION**

Blanche appears quite matter-of-fact about the deaths at Belle Reve. Is the lack of emotion in her memories of the dying a self-protective mechanism or an indication of her self-centred absorption in herself?

## TEXT 2 (SCENE 9, PAGE 72)

MITCH [*getting up*]: It's dark in here.

BLANCHE: I like it dark. The dark is comforting to me.

MITCH: I don't think I ever seen you in the light. [BLANCHE *laughs breathlessly.*] That's a fact!

BLANCHE: Is it?

MITCH: I've never seen you in the afternoon.

BLANCHE: Whose fault is that?

MITCH: You never want to go out in the afternoon.

BLANCHE: Why, Mitch, you're at the plant in the afternoon!

MITCH: Not Sunday afternoon. I've asked you to go out with me sometimes on Sundays but you always make an excuse. You never want to go out till after six and then it's always some place that's not lighted much.

BLANCHE: There is some obscure meaning in this but I fail to catch it.

MITCH: What it means is I've never had a real good look at you, Blanche.

BLANCHE: What are you leading up to?

MITCH: Let's turn the light on here.

BLANCHE [*fearfully*]: Light? Which light? What for?

MITCH: This one with the paper thing on it. [*He tears the paper lantern off the light bulb. She utters a frightened gasp.*]

BLANCHE: What did you do that for?

MITCH: So I can take a look at you good and plain!

BLANCHE: Of course you don't really mean to be insulting!

MITCH: No, just realistic.

BLANCHE: I don't want realism.

MITCH: Naw, I guess not.

BLANCHE: I'll tell you what I want. Magic! [MITCH *laughs.*] Yes, yes, magic! I try to give that to people. I misrepresent things to them. I don't tell truth, I tell what *ought* to be truth. And if that is sinful, then let me be damned for it! – *Don't turn the light on!*

**QUESTION**

The conversation between Mitch and Blanche here shows clearly how their relationship had progressed since their unsuccessful evening out in May (Scene 6). Can you identify key words and phrases establishing their relationship?

MITCH *crosses to the switch. He turns the light on and stares at her. She cries out and covers her face. He turns the light off again.*

MITCH [*slowly and bitterly*]: I don't mind you being older than what I thought. But all the rest of it – God! That pitch about your ideals being so old-fashioned and all the malarkey that you've dished out all summer. Oh, I knew you weren't sixteen any more. But I was fool enough to believe you was straight.

The subject of this passage is the final confrontation between Mitch and Blanche. She, with the premonition of disaster (heralded by the polka music she alone hears), has been drinking, and is dishevelled and confused. Mitch is in his working clothes, unshaven, and slightly drunk. In their appearance they both show their distress.

To begin with, Blanche chatters incessantly and '*laughs breathlessly*' betraying her nervousness. Mitch's monosyllabic answers are in contrast to her high-flown, artificial speeches. With statements such as 'There is some obscure meaning in this' Blanche resorts once more to the stilted educated speech of the schoolmistress in an attempt to regain control of the situation. Her flirtatiousness jars and adds to the dramatic tension. The readers (or spectators) expect an explosion of violence, which takes place in the part of the scene discussed here.

Mitch complains that the room is dark, and Blanche counters with her declaration that 'The dark is comforting to me'. The dark hides Blanche's fading beauty and, metaphorically, hides the ugliness of the cruel world around her. When Mitch tells her that he has never seen her in daylight, Blanche pretends not to understand him. In a shocking act of violence he then tears the Chinese paper lantern off the light bulb and turns the light on. We now realise that Blanche's little purchase from the Chinese shop in Scene 3 was intended by the author to play an even more important role than occasioning her revealing remark to Mitch at the poker party: 'I can't stand a naked light bulb, any more than I can a rude remark or a vulgar action' (p. 30). Its real dramatic function is to be used in a metaphor for the rape Mitch now has in mind. Stripping off the shade is a harsh, cruel action, intended to hurt and humiliate. Exposed to the harsh light Blanche cries out and covers her face while Mitch stares at her. The strong light has shown him her true appearance, and in his eyes exposed also her pretence at virtue and innocence.

Mitch's words 'good and plain' have perhaps a double meaning here: 'plain' can mean 'ugly' as well as 'clear'. Blanche's response 'you don't really mean to be insulting' shows that she is aware of the double meaning.

Emphasis on light and darkness here is striking, and we notice the reversal of conventional symbols. For Blanche light is a cruel enemy while darkness is kind. Mitch believes of course that this is simply because clear daylight will reveal that she is no longer young. This is true, but on a deeper, more important level for Blanche darkness hides the ugliness of the real world, enabling her to maintain her illusions. When her illusions go, so does her sanity.

However, Blanche is remarkably clear-headed and frank about it. She declares 'I misrepresent things … I don't tell truth, I tell what *ought* to be truth'. It is unusual for Blanche to be so frank. She is also quite clear-headed about what she does and why. Earlier, in Scene 5, she admits to Stella that she has had to pretend to be seductive, 'put a – paper lantern over the light' (p. 45). The words show that Blanche is aware of her need to camouflage reality. On that earlier occasion she used metaphors throughout, evidently because she needed to disguise the truth. Now, knowing that she has lost Mitch, she is recklessly truthful: 'then let me be damned for it!' She presents herself as an innocent girl to Mitch, because that is what he is looking for in her. More importantly perhaps, that is how she wants to see herself, though she repeatedly fails to maintain this illusion (as in her flirtation with the young man in Scene 5, and in her crude invitation to Mitch in Scene 6, fortunately spoken in French).

Mitch's use of the word 'pitch' compares Blanche's explanation to a salesman's patter and shows that her motives are lost on him. To him she is simply deceitful, a liar pretending to be virtuous. The fact that Mitch does not even remotely understand Blanche underlines the complete lack of empathy between them. Their relationship is doomed to fail sooner or later. The way they speak again stresses

> **CONTEXT**
>
> Blanche's words about trying to give people magic, the truth they want, are the only instance in the play of her speaking plainly, truthfully about herself and it is ironical that the man to whom she is speaking is quite incapable of understanding her.

the gulf between them. Blanche's high-flown, artificial language (especially in the conversation that immediately precedes the passage under discussion here) is set against Mitch's short, contemptuous (and ungrammatical) replies.

Rhetoric against grunts, soft darkness against harsh light – the message is that the relationship would have failed anyway.

# TEXT 3 (SCENE 11, PAGES 84–5)

BLANCHE [*continuing*]: What's happened here? I want an explanation of what's happened here.

STELLA [*agonizingly*]: Hush! Hush!

EUNICE: Hush! Hush! Honey.

STELLA: Please, Blanche.

BLANCHE: Why are you looking at me like that? Is something wrong with me?

EUNICE: You look wonderful, Blanche. Don't she look wonderful?

STELLA: Yes.

EUNICE: I understand you are going on a trip.

STELLA: Yes, Blanche *is*. She's going on vacation.

EUNICE: I'm green with envy.

BLANCHE: Help me, help me get dressed!

STELLA [*handing her dress*]: Is this what you –

BLANCHE: Yes, it will do! I'm anxious to get out of here – this place is a trap!

EUNICE: What a pretty blue jacket.

STELLA: It's lilac coloured.

BLANCHE: You're both mistaken. It's Della Robbia blue. The blue of the robe in the old Madonna pictures. Are these grapes washed?

*She fingers the bunch of grapes which* EUNICE *has brought in.*

EUNICE: Huh?

BLANCHE: Washed, I said. Are they washed?

EUNICE: They're from the French Market.

**CONTEXT**

The disjointed trivia of this conversation prepare the audience for the reality of Blanche's 'vacation', the mental hospital to which her sister has her committed. Here the dramatic irony is revealed only gradually.

BLANCHE: That doesn't mean they've been washed. [*The cathedral bells chime.*] Those cathedral bells – they're the only clean thing in the Quarter. Well, I'm going now. I'm ready to go.

EUNICE [*whispering*]: She's going to walk out before they get here.

STELLA: Wait, Blanche.

BLANCHE: I don't want to pass in front of those men.

EUNICE: Then wait'll the game breaks up.

STELLA: Sit down and …

BLANCHE *turns weakly, hesitantly about. She lets them push her into a chair.*

BLANCHE: I can smell the sea air. The rest of my time I'm going to spend on the sea. And when I die, I'm going to die on the sea. You know what I shall die of? [*She plucks a grape.*] I shall die of eating an unwashed grape one day out on the ocean. I will die – with my hand in the hand of some nice-looking ship's doctor, a very young one with a small blond moustache and a big silver watch. "Poor lady," they'll say, "the quinine did her no good. That unwashed grape has transported her soul to heaven." [*The cathedral chimes are heard.*] And I'll be buried at sea sewn up in a clean white sack and dropped overboard – at noon – in the blaze of summer – and into an ocean as blue as [*chimes again*] my first lover's eyes!

**QUESTION**

There is pathos in Blanche's daydream of a death at sea, pictured in crystal colours as in a romance novel. Again we are aware of the cruel contrast between this daydream and reality. Is it successful as an appeal for sympathy and pity for the heroine of the play?

The last passage has an extraordinary dramatic force. On the surface it is a scene of domestic activity; Stella packing Blanche's trunk, Eunice gossiping, Blanche emerging from the bathroom. The group of poker players seen through the portières in the kitchen, however, is ominously quiet, in deliberate contrast to their rowdiness in Scene 3.

The audience (and readers) are in ignorance of the meaning of the scene at first, like Blanche herself. There is complicity binding together Stella and Eunice, and the players, all of whom know what is going to happen.

Blanche's agitated question 'What's happened here?' shows that she senses that something momentous is happening. She is aware of the tension and is frightened. From the words 'Is something wrong with me?' Blanche reveals her awareness of the involuntary scrutiny by the other two women who know what is about to befall her. The euphemisms 'going on a trip ... going on vacation' are cruelly ironical. Blanche's 'Help me, help me get dressed!' is a thinly disguised plea for help as she feels she is caught in a trap. The other two women chatter on, flattering Blanche, complimenting her on her outfit. This is very effective as a piece of theatre as the conventional small talk somehow emphasises the underlying tension.

**QUESTION**

Are the images of virginal purity and cleanliness in this passage successful in underlining the reality of Blanche's position in ironical contrast?

The talk succeeds in distracting Blanche a little. Like a true schoolmistress she offers information about the correct name for the shade of blue of her jacket. The image of the Virgin Mary is of course one of purity, of virginity, and this reference is ironical for Blanche. She remains on edge, however, and her unease finds expression in her impatient, rather offhand remarks to Eunice: 'Washed, I said ... That doesn't mean they've been washed'.

Blanche admits now that she is aware of the silent presence of the poker players, and fears them. The trauma she suffered at the hands of Mitch, and especially Stanley, has made her afraid.

When she allows herself to be seated in a chair, Blanche's thought about unwashed grapes starts her on an extraordinary flight of fancy of her death at sea, caused by eating an unwashed grape. She sees her own death in brilliantly clear colours, a pretty scene quite unlike what she had repeatedly witnessed at Belle Reve.

The sketch of the young ship's doctor who will be by her side is strikingly detailed, idealised somewhat in the style of romantic fiction. He offers an ironic contrast to the real doctor from the mental hospital who will presently arrive to take her away. Perhaps this daydream of a pretty death with a handsome doctor beside her has prepared her to accept and trust the real doctor when he comes. The tone of romantic fiction is maintained through to the end of her speech: 'an ocean as blue as ... my first lover's eyes'.

We notice also the emphasis on the purity of tone of the cathedral bells which are heard in the apartment for the first time now. The pure tone of the bell, the clean white sack in which she imagines herself buried at sea, both symbolise her longing for purification, for a cleansing from her sins, as did her frequent long baths. In the context, however, her dream of purity and of a peaceful death takes on an ironical meaning: the voyage she will undertake on the arm of the hospital doctor will take her to the harsh ugliness of a mental institution, an incarceration that will be a living death for her.

Her imaginary voyage set against the fast approaching reality gives the scene its painful tension. Throughout her speech she is answered by the unspoken thoughts of the others present in a dramatic counterpoint. This scene offers a splendid example of the dramatist's skill.

**CONTEXT**

The phrase 'silence speaks volumes' sums up this scene: Blanche's nervous chatter and her dreamy description of her death at sea are given their full dramatic weight by the silence of the other players.

## PART THREE

## CRITICAL APPROACHES

# CHARACTERISATION

The characterisation in the *text* of a play is quite a different matter from the characterisation in a stage production. When we see a stage performance most of our work is done for us: we see the setting, what the persons in a play look like, and to a considerable extent we are made to see them as the director and the cast conceive them to be. When we read the text of a play, however, we must use our imagination and form our own idea, however nebulous, of the appearance and character of the persons in the play. Here we shall consider how we learn to imagine the action of *A Streetcar Named Desire* on the basis of a simple list of characters and the author's stage directions.

As to the stage directions: readers will have noticed at the start of Scene 1 the detailed description of the stage set, which combines practical details of the appearance of the houses with skilful poetic evocations of the atmosphere: '*the warm breath of the brown river*', the '*peculiarly tender blue*' of the sky. Equally evocative are, for instance, the stage directions at the start of Scene 3.

The descriptions of the main characters in the stage directions make for interesting reading. On her first appearance Blanche is described in some detail, and we are made aware of the unsuitability of her outfit for the rundown street where her sister lives. Later on (Scene 9) we may recall the playwright's ominous words in the stage directions that she '*must avoid a strong light*' (p. 5) which will show her true age. She is compared to a moth, a comparison that stresses her vulnerability.

The description of Stanley later in this scene concentrates on his sexual power, his readiness to enjoy the good things of life, his self-confidence. Of his physical appearance we learn nothing apart from his height and his compact build. Nothing much is said about Stella, '*a gentle young woman*' (p. 4), about twenty-five years old, of a different background from her husband.

**QUESTION**

Blanche is described in the stage directions in terms of her appearance, while the description of Stanley emphasises his character. Can you think of a reason for this?

The last of the foursome of main actors, Mitch remains a shadowy figure, except for his brief description of himself in Scene 6, which betrays his dullness but tells us little else.

The brevity of these descriptions offers freedom to the director and cast to create the characters from the scraps of information given by the dramatist.

What of the readers? They too are given the freedom to endow the main characters with faces and figures, peculiarities of gesture and walk, though inevitably these will be shadowy figures, lacking the definition of real actors on the stage.

Throughout the play Williams emphasises the way in which people's natures cause them to act in a particular way. The inevitability of fate – the streetcar that carries them – is brought about by the characters being what they are, acting as they do because their natures compel them. To say this is to stress the importance of character in the play. The dramatist's skill lies in taking the human qualities necessary for the enactment of the tragedy, and building from them, through speech and action, believable human beings.

> **CONTEXT**
>
> Williams stresses the role of character in a person's actions: the streetcar – or fate – that carries them is their own making.

## BLANCHE

To begin with, the characters appearing in Scene 1 are dismissed with only brief description (if any) of their appearance. When Blanche appears, however, she is described in more detail – not only her clothes, but also the impression she gives of delicacy and vulnerability.

As we read on, her appearance becomes ever clearer and so does her character. Her appearance – slim figure, a face of delicate, fading beauty – is described in the stage directions, and the readers also gather further information about her from the other characters' comments. (Indeed she demands flattering comments from her sister, from the reluctant Stanley and from Eunice.)

Her complex, contradictory character also becomes clear. Very early in the play we become aware of her class snobbery (in her dismissal of the black neighbour's kindness and of Eunice's company) and we shall be reminded of it again in the last scene when she rudely dismisses Eunice's gift of grapes with her obsessional concern about cleanliness.

**CONTEXT**

Blanche's complex character is built up through the dialogue as well as by her actions throughout the play.

We also learn that she is a heavy drinker. The reasons for her craving for alcohol are implied as we learn about her guilt for her husband's suicide and about her promiscuity. Alcohol offers temporary amnesia and reassurance. Equally, her passion for taking long baths should be taken as a symbol of her yearning to wash away her guilt. (Of course, it has a dramatic function as well, her long absences in the bathroom enabling the other characters to speak of matters that are not for her ears.)

Stanley gives us the full details of her past later on, but her cheap seductive manner noted by him with astonishment in Scene 2 and again in Scene 3 is an early warning. As she so primly insists on her respectability to Mitch in Scene 6, readers will inevitably recall her flirting with Stanley earlier, as well as the episode with the young man in Scene 5. Here her character is revealed through her actions, leaving the readers to draw their own conclusions.

The readers – and the audience in the theatre – will be struck by the inconsistencies in her behaviour: her cultural pretensions are designed to impress people with her superiority, and stand in contrast to her genuine love of poetry. She is wilfully ignorant of the causes of the loss of Belle Reve, yet she understands that the root cause was the profligacy of her family, their cavalier attitude to money. These inconsistencies contribute to make her character less predictable and more fully human.

In her conversation with her sister in Scene 4, Blanche admits obliquely that she knows about sexual desire – 'when the devil is in you' (p. 40) – but it seems that she has never experienced true passion in which love and sexual desire play equal parts. Her incomprehension of real passion is total and will play a part in alienating her sister. The full strength of Stella's love for her husband is shown in the last scene, when she will have her sister committed to a mental hospital, rather than believe the truth about the rape.

Passion like this is beyond Blanche's imagining, and it may be that she is too absorbed in herself ever to surrender herself. Self-absorption also explains her inability to understand the effects of her behaviour. After the row with Stanley in Scene 2, she reassures her sister that she 'handled it nicely' (p. 23), yet this is the very point at which Stanley begins to be suspicious about his sister-in-law's past history.

Blanche may hide her alcoholism behind her euphemisms but she does recognise some of her weaknesses – 'I've got to be good and keep my hands off children' (Scene 5, p. 49). The weakness that she never does admit, and may not be aware of, is the reckless streak in her, which makes her risk her chance of security, in the episode with the young man in Scene 5 and, repeatedly, when entertaining Mitch in Scene 6.

Significantly she never speaks of this except when telling herself to be good: her actions on the stage alone speak here. Perhaps this is because she herself is uncertain about her motives for such behaviour. The readers too can only speculate, and it is arguable that the uncertainty about some aspects of Blanche's character may well contribute to making her a believable human being.

Williams himself apparently came to see her as a real woman who went on living outside his play. He remarked later that Blanche was a real survivor and that he was sure that she would recover and leave the asylum and marry a 'Gentleman Caller' (Tennessee Williams' title of a film script, later his play *The Glass Menagerie*).

**QUESTION**

Do you think it is quite usual for an author to see a character in his/her work as a real person?

## STANLEY

Williams does not build up Stanley Kowalski's character in exactly the same way as that of Blanche. There is little physical description of him: '*of medium height ... strongly, compactly built*' (Scene 1, p. 13). Instead Williams concentrates on the impact Stanley has on those around him. His intense masculinity, his awareness of his sexual magnetism are at the core of his personality, and other aspects of it spring from this pride in his sexual magnetism, his ability to attract and satisfy women. Williams has a striking phrase for him: '*the gaudy seed-bearer*' (p. 14), the cock of the walk. His gaudy bowling shirt and his wedding-night pyjamas are his

**QUESTION**

Did Tennessee
Williams sacrifice
subtlety of
characterisation to
the demands of
the plot in his
portrait of the
sexually arrogant
Stanley?

plumage. He is at ease with the men round him, confident of his
own superiority to them. He bullies them and they respond with
loyalty and affection. For women he has nothing but contempt,
seeing them as easy game. His basic contempt for women may be
gathered from the way he addresses the sisters during the poker
game in Scene 3: 'You hens cut out that conversation in there!'
(p. 27). He abuses his friends as well, but they respond with loyalty
and even affection.

Stanley's machismo and his need to dominate, so blatantly shown
during the poker party in Scene 3, are the aspects of this character
stressed throughout the play, perhaps in order to make the rape
more credible.

Stanley's ungrammatical speech betrays his lack of education, but he
is shrewd, sensing quite early in his acquaintance with Blanche that
her behaviour is sometimes quite out of keeping with the character
of a Southern lady. He is quite as acutely class-conscious as Blanche
herself. Having married a gentlewoman, he is resentful of the
differences in outlook and manner between himself and his wife,
and knows that pulling her down to his level is part of his sexual
attraction for her. Conflict is therefore inevitable between him and
Blanche, who is trying to make Stella revert to the past of Belle
Reve. It is equally inevitable, given Stanley's awareness of his
masculinity and his contempt for women, that he should seek to
express his hostility to Blanche through sexual domination.

The way the play has been constructed, with the rape as the climax
in the penultimate scene, and the last scene centred on Blanche's
tragic fate, influences our perception of Stanley. In spite of his
blustering bravado, he is a sadly diminished figure in that last scene.
Blanche fears him still, yet she goes out without a backward glance
at either her sister or her brother-in-law. We leave Stanley as he tries
to re-establish his domination over his wife in the only way he
knows, by making love to her.

Our altered perception of Stanley in the last scene may be seen as a
testimony to the dramatist's skill. Though his character is
unchanged, we see him differently, as do perhaps the others in the

play. Their actions and reactions continue to occupy our thoughts beyond the confines of the play. Such speculations, which go beyond the time and place of the play, are surely proof of the spectators' or readers' emotional involvement, and may be seen as the highest compliment they can pay to the dramatist.

## STELLA

We are not given much direct information about Stella's appearance or character. The stage directions describe her as '*a gentle young woman ... of a background obviously quite different from her husband's*' (Scene 1, p. 4). We learn a little more about her from the characters' comments, especially Blanche's. She remarks on Stella's quiet, reserved manner. Stella's reply that she never had much of a chance to talk with her sister around, though, hints at an independence of mind. A certain dry, sarcastic note may be heard as she speaks, but her sister never notices it. Blanche treats her like a child, a 'blessed baby', ordering her to stand up (Scene 1, p. 8), rebuking her for her untidiness. Stella makes no objection to this, but it is noticeable that any adverse comment on her husband brings an instant protest.

Stella's silent manner is her response to what is of no importance to her. It is obvious, even without her passionate declaration in Scene 4, that she is deeply in love with her husband, and this love is the cornerstone of her existence. We need to be convinced of her devotion to her husband if we are to accept as believable her complicity in Blanche's committal. To do otherwise, to accept that her sister is sane, would mean accepting also Blanche's accusation of Stanley. If the choice lies between her sister and her husband, there is no question whom she will choose.

 **CHECK THE FILM**
Bowing to Hollywood pressure, Kazan's film version ends with Stella leaving Stanley. This solution makes nonsense of Stella's passion for her husband.

Stella does care for her family: she is distressed when she hears of the loss of Belle Reve; she weeps when Blanche accuses her of indifference to the fate of her family; and she weeps bitterly when Blanche is taken to the mental hospital. Her '*luxurious*' sobbing (Scene 11, p. 89) will not change anything; though as Williams' choice of adjective implies, this is an indulgence peripheral to her decision.

Based upon an overpowering physical passion, Stella's surrender to Stanley is almost total: she has accepted his world and its values. She has chosen to become part of Stanley's life, perhaps gradually remembering less and less of her early life, and accepting her husband's standards (her reading a comic in bed is symptomatic of this), becoming more and more like him.

We have spoken above of characters taking on a life of their own beyond the confines of the play. When it comes to Stella and Stanley we may be permitted to wonder whether the semi-comic characters of Eunice and Steve were introduced to foreshadow the Kowalskis in years to come – Stella slovenly, fat and blowzy after too many pregnancies, and Stanley no longer the '*gaudy seed-bearer*' (Scene 1, p. 14) but a corpulent, wheezing patron of the local prostitutes.

We may be confident that Stella will carry a burden of guilt (as Tennessee Williams accepted his imagined share of responsibility for his sister's lobotomy and subsequent committal) as a price to be paid for the preservation of her marriage.

## MITCH

**CONTEXT**

Though the least important of the four chief characters, Mitch plays a significant part in the development of the plot.

In the interplay of characters in *A Streetcar Named Desire* Mitch too has a part to play. Shy, clumsy, slow-thinking, he acts as a foil to the shrewd, loud, domineering Stanley, as well as to the poetry-loving, fanciful Blanche with her cultural aspirations. His role is to offer Blanche the promise of a safe haven, to spur Stanley indirectly to find out about Blanche's past in order to protect his old buddy. Also, as Williams hints in Scene 3, Mitch's interest in Blanche encourages Stanley to think of her as sexually desirable, yet another factor in the catastrophic events of Scene 10.

Mitch matters to Stanley: Stanley needs his admiration and respect and is unwilling to relinquish his hold on him. This jealousy pays a part in Stanley's determination to expose Blanche and so regain his domination of Mitch. That he is to be seen as Stanley's shadow is shown in his tearing of the paper lantern, and in his half-hearted attempt at raping Blanche. Both these actions are repeated by Stanley, the successfully accomplished rape actually later the same night. The harshness of his action shocks like a rape, and ironically his own half-hearted attempt at raping Blanche fails, and his hero Stanley carries out the act the same night.

We are given no physical description of Mitch in the stage directions. The only details of his appearance – tall, 'a heavy build' (Scene 6, p. 52), perspiring easily – are given by himself in Scene 6, as part of his laborious attempt at conversation. Like his physical appearance, his character is never fully described by the others. The depiction of Mitch's character depends almost entirely on our reactions to his behaviour.

Though perhaps not 'a natural gentleman' (p. 54), as Blanche describes him in Scene 6, he seems gentler, kinder than the others. He is devoted to his ailing mother, and therefore the butt of Stanley's jokes. He is dull-witted and incapable of understanding Blanche's explanation of her past behaviour. He clings to the facts he had checked out and, hardly surprisingly perhaps, rejects her with contempt.

Although Mitch is perhaps not as central to the play as some of the others, his behaviour is important for the depiction not only of his character, but also of those around him.

## THEMES

All three major themes of *A Streetcar Named Desire* reflect Williams' own private terrors, and this gives the edge to his writing.

### DESIRE AND FATE

The theme that dominates the play is contained in its arresting and memorable title. There really was a streetcar in New Orleans that carried the word 'Desire' as its destination, and another that went to 'Cemeteries'. Blanche's journey, first to Desire and then to Cemeteries, sums up her life, driven by a sexual passion and finally ending up in the 'living death' of the asylum. When Tennessee Williams was living in New Orleans in 1946, and was working on *A Streetcar Named Desire,* he was so struck by the names of these two streetcars that he mentioned them in an essay he wrote at the time: 'Their indiscourageable progress up and down Royal Street struck me as having some symbolic bearing of a broad nature on the life in the Vieux Carré – and everywhere else for that matter' (quoted in *The Kindness of Strangers: The Life of Tennessee Williams* by

**QUESTION**

Do you think the title of the play offers a full and satisfactory summary of the tragedy presented?

Donald Spoto, p. 129). From the theatrical point of view, of course, such a title was pure gold.

A streetcar running unswervingly along the rails to its destination could be seen as a symbol of the inexorability of fate. To Tennessee Williams, however, the streetcar's destination, 'Desire', carried a more specific meaning. Not just an undefined fatal force, it symbolised a particularly destructive power, that of sexual passion. In Scene 4 (p. 40), when the sisters speak of sexual desire, Blanche uses the same image of 'that rattle-trap street-car'. Stella ripostes, 'Haven't you ever ridden on that street-car?' and 'It brought me here' is Blanche's bitter reply. Talking in metaphors, they both know what they are talking about – and so did the author himself. The quotation from the fifth stanza of Hart Crane's poem 'The Broken Tower', which Williams uses as the **epigraph** to *A Streetcar Named Desire*, sums up the misery of promiscuity both for Blanche and for the dramatist himself: 'not for long to hold each desperate choice'.

Like Blanche, Tennessee Williams was driven throughout his life from one sexual encounter to another, and again like Blanche he too seemed incapable of committing himself to a permanent relationship (see **Background** on **Tennessee Williams**). When Blanche longs for Mitch to marry her, she is not seeking a permanent sexual relationship but the material security of a home of her own: 'The poor man's Paradise – is a little peace' (Scene 9, p. 73).

To be driven by desire, Williams seems to be saying, is self-destructive, yet the victims, whether of one overpowering passion or of the thrill of a string of promiscuous encounters, are carried along helplessly, unable to escape. Blanche's fate is foreordained, and the playwright stresses this in the streetcar image. Her encounter with the young man just before Mitch's arrival (Scene 5) and her reckless acting out of a French prostitute's invitation (Scene 6) are a part of her nature, seeming to ensure that she will not become the contented housewife she hopes to be.

The force of desire drives Stella too, who has abandoned herself – and her integrity – to her passion for Stanley. What the final

**CHECK THE BOOK**

Hart Crane (1899–1932) was an American poet much influenced by Walt Whitman. His best-known poem 'The Bridge' is a symbolic celebration of old and new America.

**QUESTION**

Is the quotation from Hart Crane a fitting epigraph for the whole play *A Streetcar Named Desire* – and for its author?

destination of her streetcar ride might be is not shown – except
perhaps in Eunice.

Curiously, there is another, similar symbol of fate in this play, one
with a very respectable literary lineage. In Scenes 4, 6 and 10
Williams introduces a roaring locomotive at a dramatic moment
(Blanche's condemnation of Stanley in Scene 4; her description of
her husband's suicide in Scene 6; and just before the rape in Scene
10). The random introduction of the locomotive as a symbol does
not carry the impact of the streetcar image, though other writers
have used it with considerable effect – Leo Tolstoy in *Anna
Karenina* (1875–7) and Emile Zola in *La Bête Humaine* (1890).

It may be that Tennessee Williams had originally intended to follow
these other writers and use the locomotive as the **leitmotiv** of his
play, but was so struck by the irony of a lurching streetcar in New
Orleans with the grand name 'Desire' that he abandoned his original
plan.

# DEATH

In Williams' mind, the streetcar to Desire was linked with another
going to Cemeteries. This fortuitous link was to him a logical
sequence, with early death the outcome of a life driven by passion.

Williams' obsessive terror of death could perhaps be traced back to
a near-fatal childhood illness, but it was to remain with him always.
In 1946 he became convinced that he was dying of an incurable
pancreatic cancer (his beloved grandmother died of the disease in
1943) and it seems likely that Blanche's obsession with death was
rooted in the author's own. In his later years it took the form of
hypochondria of a very intense form. Ironically, it might be said
that this hypochondria killed him: he choked to death on a
barbiturate pill.

In *A Streetcar* Blanche remembers vividly the ghastly deaths that
she had to witness at Belle Reve, as her elderly relations died one by
one, with no one to nurse them except herself. Her memories of that
time are with her always: first Stella (Scene 1) and then Mitch (Scene
6) are made to listen to her recollections. She gives enough

**CHECK
THE FILM**
The film version
opens with a shot of
a roaring
locomotive
announcing
Blanche's arrival in
New Orleans.
Evidently it has no
other significance.

gruesome detail to make the impact of death felt – there is the dying woman so swollen by disease that her body could not be fitted into a coffin, but had to be 'burned like rubbish' (Scene 1, p. 12); and the 'blood-stained pillow-slips' (Scene 10, p. 74) which Blanche had to change because there were no longer any servants. It is not by chance that Blanche dreams of being buried 'at sea sewn up in a clean white sack' (Scene 11, p. 85). Her romanticising instinct recoils from the reality of death, but the obsessive thought of death is there always.

The significant death that is ever present in Blanche's mind is the suicide of her young husband, for which she knows herself to be responsible. Signalled by the music of the Varsouviana polka, which she danced with her husband on the night of his death, the events of that night play in her mind like a film, always ending with the shot that killed him. The audience hear all this – and the readers have the stage directions – yet in a curious variant of the **aside**, the other players on the stage hear nothing. Their inability to participate in this tragedy makes Blanche's memories peculiarly private and contributes to her isolation.

The reminders of death throughout the play culminate in the symbolic figure of the Mexican seller of flowers for the dead (Scene 9). This figure plays a similar part to the grotesque shadows surrounding Blanche in Scene 10. The realism of the earlier scenes is abandoned in order to give these symbolic figures the prominence that Tennessee Williams gave them in his own mind. No longer the Grim Reaper on the doorstep of Belle Reve, but an old woman whispering insidiously, death was present in Williams' own mind quite as much as in his play.

## MADNESS

Blanche's fear of madness is first hinted at in Scene 1: 'I *can't* be *alone*! Because – as you must have noticed – I'm – *not* very *well* …' (p. 10). Never stable even as a girl, she was shattered by the circumstances of her husband's death and by the part she played in it. The harrowing deaths at Belle Reve with which she evidently had to cope on her own, also took their toll. By this time she had begun her descent into promiscuity and alcoholism. Stella's remark that Blanche's behaviour caused distress at home (Scene 7) indicates that

Blanche's deterioration began earlier, while her parents were still alive. As her promiscuity increased and she drank more, she began to create her fantasy world of adoring, respectful admirers, of romantic songs and fun parties.

It seems doubtful whether she was ever entirely successful in creating this dream world: the memories of her husband's suicide are never entirely absent from her thoughts. As the sound of the polka grows louder in her mind, the revolver shot puts a temporary end to it. She comes to wait for the sound of the shot to relieve her of the nightmare, if only temporarily. It seems that she has learned to live with this, as she remarks to Mitch in a matter-of-fact way, 'There now, the shot! It always stops after that!' (Scene 9, p. 71). In a way, this practical way of dealing with a nightmare is truly terrifying, as she accommodates the terrors into her daily life.

 **QUESTION**

Does Blanche have more trouble dealing with her recurring nightmares, or with the ugly reality of the outside world?

Stanley's revelations of Blanche's past (which force her to confront it), Mitch's rejection of her as a liar who is 'not clean enough' (Scene 10, p. 75), his contemptuous attempt at raping her, and finally Stanley's violation of her – all these brutal acts break her and her mind gives way. She retreats from the unbearable reality into her make-believe world, making her committal to an institution possible, even inevitable.

Like the other major themes of the play – desire, fate and death – madness too was Williams' obsession. He was afraid that he might go mad because of his sister Rose, whose strange behaviour had long been a source of anxiety to her parents (the anxieties of the family over Blanche at Belle Reve echo this). Rose experienced violent sexual fantasies and made accusations against her father. To avoid scandal, Rose's parents had her committed to a mental hospital and consented to a pre-frontal lobotomy (standard practice at the time). Rose calmed down as a result, but was left with no memories, no mind. The effect on Tennessee Williams was shattering. Not only did he feel guilty because, being absent from home, he did nothing to prevent the operation, but he also feared that Rose's mental illness might be hereditary and that he too might lose his sanity. He certainly did have some sort of mental breakdown in his early twenties, which contributed to his anxieties later on.

## DRAMATIC TECHNIQUES

### THE UNITIES

**QUESTION**

The unities – help or hindrance to the playwright?

The convention of imposing rules on playwrights is a long-held tradition. The so-called three **unities** – of time (demanding that the action of a play should take place within twenty-four hours), of place (requiring the setting to remain the same throughout the play) and of action (never so clearly defined as the other two unities, this was an insistence that the play should centre on the main characters, with no sub-plots, and that the action should have a satisfying ending) – were wrongly attributed by Renaissance literary critics to Aristotle, the Greek philosopher and critic. Whilst Aristotle observed that contemporary Greek tragedies concentrated on one complete action usually taking place within twenty-four hours, he never laid down the strict rules that much later became known as the three unities.

From the fifteenth century onwards the three unities were discussed by critics, and observed – or broken (notably by Shakespeare) – by dramatists. Though not strictly adhered to, these rules still provided a framework within which a playwright could build a play.

**CHECK THE BOOK**

All these dramatists are readily available in paperback editions (see **Further reading**).

During his years at the University of Missouri and at Washington University, Tennessee Williams read avidly, especially the modern European dramatists – August Strindberg, Henrik Ibsen and Anton Chekhov – all of whom wrote plays centred on a single character, which of course ensured the unity of action. (The other two unities had over the centuries lost their significance.)

If we look at *A Streetcar Named Desire*, the first thing to strike us is the unity of place, the entire action taking place in the Kowalskis' apartment or just outside it. The events in the play stretch over several months, starting in May, and reaching their climax in September, with the tragic aftermath happening some weeks later.

The play centres on Blanche Dubois, and the other actors' significance lies in the way their behaviour will affect her. Her sister offers kindness and hospitality, but only as far as her all-absorbing passion for her husband allows. Ultimately, however guilt-struck, she will sacrifice her sister to save her marriage.

Stanley resents Blanche as an intruder in a close, passionate sexual relationship; and she reminds him of his wife's superior background, representing values that he cannot and will not appreciate. Instinctively he sees Blanche as an enemy and sets out to drive her away. Given his character – and Blanche's – the antagonism between them is sexual in nature, and the act of violence through which Stanley destroys Blanche is to him a triumph of his sexuality. To Blanche it is the ultimate breaking up of her dream world, which will wreck her sanity.

The play, then, presents the downfall of a weak woman who will rise to a tragic dignity in the end. By focusing on Blanche, Williams might be said to achieve a unity of action. Like many other playwrights, Williams disregards the artificiality of the unity of time and instinctively adopts the unities of place and action.

**QUESTION**

Can you think of another modern play with a similar outline?

## STRUCTURE

Distinct from the theoretical rules of the unities there are certain practical considerations to which dramatists must pay attention.

Amongst these is the attention span of the audience. Trivial as this sounds, it is a serious consideration if the dramatist is to hold his audience. There have been exceptionally long plays, such as Shakespeare's *Henry IV, Parts I and II* (1597), if the two parts are performed together, or Eugene O'Neill's *Long Day's Journey into Night* (1956), but very long plays are rare.

As a concession to both the attention span of the audience and the physical stamina of the cast, the convention developed of dividing plays into acts.

In Elizabethan tragedy there were no stage sets, the author's words providing a verbal picture of the background. Changes of setting were therefore easy. With the arrival of painted scenery and realistic props in the eighteenth and nineteenth centuries, changes of setting became technically quite difficult and also costly. Authors were now expected to limit settings to a few, each change of scenery dictating the length of an act.

Of course nowadays advanced lighting techniques and a revolving stage offer the possibility of doing away with the conventional division into acts, yet the convention persists to a large extent.

Williams divided *A Streetcar Named Desire* into eleven scenes, with no break for an interval indicated. Inevitably there have been speculations on his reasons for this. It has been suggested that Williams chose this unconventional structure because he felt that his particular talent was for writing short one-act plays, and that he could not sustain dramatic tension for three acts of conventional length. Certainly if we examine the eleven scenes in *A Streetcar Named Desire* we find that every one of them ends with a punchline or a dramatic gesture. For example, in Scene 1 Blanche sinks back, her head in her arms, to be sick; and Steve's laconic statement, 'This game is a seven-card stud' closes the play. The effect in each case is that of the ending of a playlet, with the players motionless in a ***tableau vivant***.

Indeed, it is difficult to see how the play could have been divided into three acts, as only a few of the scenes, (2–3, perhaps 7–8 and 9–10) take place within the same time span.

The concept of a series of one-act playlets is reinforced by the element of repetition in the play. The deaths at Belle Reve, the death of Blanche's husband, her fear of growing old, her passion for baths: all these are dramatically necessary in more than one scene. Although they are presented from different angles, yet the repetitions will strengthen the impression that these scenes stand independent of one another.

The fairly rapid shifts of focus in *A Streetcar* may remind us of another art form – the cinema. We can almost see the camera witnessing one incident and moving on to another, taking in a whole scene or focusing on one face. We should remember that Tennessee Williams grew up in the twenties and thirties, the golden age of Hollywood cinema. We should remember too that he was the film critic for his high school magazine, paying close attention to the films he was reviewing, and consciously or unconsciously absorbing the techniques used.

Apart from presentation, most of Williams' plays share with the cinema their melodramatic elements, the use of sensational scenes of violence and passion. The adaptability of Williams' plays for the screen was certainly not lost on Hollywood: no fewer than fifteen of his plays were made into films, with Williams himself collaborating on the scripts for seven of them.

## HANDLING OF TIME

The action of the play covers a period of some five months. The first six scenes stretch over the first few days of Blanche's visit in May, but Scene 7 moves abruptly to mid September; and Scenes 7 to 10 all take place within one day. The last scene follows a few weeks later.

In other words, there is a cluster of dramatic events in May and another, more dramatic, in September. By this time, some relationships have crystallised: Stanley dislikes Blanche as an intruder and a potential rival with both Stella and Mitch; Mitch is hesitantly courting Blanche. By September, some of the obscure references to the past have become clear too: the loss of Belle Reve; the suicide of Blanche's husband and the reasons for it; the reason for Blanche's departure from Laurel; her hopeless material and emotional situation.

**QUESTION**

You will notice that Scenes 7–10 observe the unity of time, compressing several violent actions with far reaching consequences into a single day. Does the unity of time contribute significantly to the dramatic effect?

The first group of scenes sets the stage for the calamities that will take place in the second group, and the last scene, which takes place some weeks later, shows the outcome of these events. We have touched on the possible reasons for Tennessee Williams' choice of eleven short scenes instead of the conventional three to five acts (see **Structure**, above). It might also be useful to consider here the grouping of the scenes into two clusters, with the last scene set apart both in mood and in tension.

Though Scenes 1–6 set the stage for the second cluster of scenes, their function cannot be said to be purely preparatory. Dramatic incidents, violence and passion figure in all of them in varying degrees. There is perhaps a sense of restraint in the first group

**CONTEXT**

While the first six scenes move more slowly, the violent events of Scenes 7–10 follow at a faster rate. The speed of action might be said to play a dramatic part here.

(except for the Stanley's drunken rage in Scene 3 which can be accepted as part of the usual pattern for his poker nights), of waiting for what the future will bring. The anticipation of disaster is muted, but the audience (or readers) are already aware that there will be no happy ending.

In the second cluster of scenes (Scenes 7– 10), Tennessee Williams makes it quite clear that, as Blanche says in Scene 10, 'Some awful thing will happen' (p. 81). In Scene 7 we hear Stanley's denunciation of Blanche and her contrapuntal singing offstage, in blissful ignorance of what is being said about her. The tension culminates in Scene 8 with Stanley's cruel birthday present of a bus ticket back to Laurel. In Scene 9 the symbolic – one might say **Expressionist** – figure of the Mexican flower-seller appears, reminding Blanche of all the deaths in her past. It is followed by Mitch's attempt to rape her. The audience or readers may be alerted by this abortive attempt as to what is going to happen in Scene 10. The scene begins amicably enough, with Stanley even offering to 'bury the hatchet' (p. 77), but soon the tone of the conversation and the atmosphere changes. As Stanley strips off Blanche's pretensions, menacing shapes appear on the walls of the apartment and inhuman voices are heard. The back walls become transparent and scenes of sordid violence are seen in the street outside. The appalling climax of the scene is now inevitable, anticipated by Blanche's terror.

The differences between the two groups of scenes, then, lie in the degree of hostility and violence that they present. The first group could be seen as Act I, (albeit a long one) establishing the characters and the relationships between them, outlining the possibilities for potential conflict.

The second group might be regarded as a violent Act II, in which the expected violent events take place. Going against dramatic conventions, the climax of the play takes place at the close of the last scene of this second cluster.

Scene 11, as a short Act III, presents the aftermath of Scene 10's climax but it is just as shocking, as the frantic Blanche struggles to hold on to her shattered dreams and emerges triumphant.

Time is used as a dramatic device in the sequence of eleven scenes. The first six follow one another quite slowly, the next four shorter scenes move at greater speed, thereby creating the tension of a violent and tragic climax. The last scene maintains the illusion of humdrum everyday activities which is shattered by Blanche's struggle to escape, followed by the restored illusion of calm.

Although at varying speed, the eleven scenes follow one another in chronological order, but some significant features of the plot – in particular, Blanche's promiscuity, her drinking and her part in the loss of Belle Reve – are not given in any logical order, but through oblique references throughout the play (see **Extended commentary** on **Text 1**).

## VISUAL AND SOUND EFFECTS

The visual aspect of *A Streetcar Named Desire* was clearly very important to the author, partly perhaps as a result of his interest in the cinema (see **Structure**, above). His stage directions are quite detailed, using evocative imagery to convey how the dramatist envisaged the scene. The intention was to create an atmosphere that would heighten the impact of the action – so that you could almost say that the apartment in Elysian Fields is one of the actors in the play.

That the visual aspect of a stage presentation was important to Williams is shown with particular clarity in the stage directions for Scene 3, which specify the vivid colours of the men's shirts, the yellow linoleum, the green lamp shade, and refer to a Van Gogh painting of a billiard-parlour. Scene 9 employs the symbolic figure of the Mexican flower-seller as a portent of death; while Scene 10 uses **Expressionist** menacing shapes inside the apartment, and scenes of violence outside, to reflect Blanche's terror.

Sound effects are similarly employed to convey an atmosphere: there is the blue piano with the vague message of the indomitable, pleasure-loving spirit of the quarter; the Varsouviana polka which calls up and accompanies Blanche's guilty memories of her husband; and perhaps also the roar of the locomotive in Scenes 4, 6 and 10 – though its function is less clearly defined and it has no dramatic

**QUESTION**

Do you think the emphasis on colour in the stage directions for Scene 3 was inspired by the author's recollection of a painting?

purpose except to enable Stanley to eavesdrop on Blanche in Scene 4.

**CHECK THE FILM**

In the film version of *A Streetcar Named Desire*, music plays a much less important part, perhaps to avoid dealing with the problem of technical presentation.

The only sound effect with a specific function is the Varsouviana polka and the revolver that silences it. What distinguishes them from the other sound effects is that Blanche alone can hear them, an aspect that is very difficult to convey either on that stage or on the printed page. Only Mitch's question 'What music?' (Scene 9, p. 70) tries to put across the message that the polka plays in Blanche's mind only. Williams tries to deal with the technical problem of presentation here; the truth is that there is no satisfactory method to deal with the problem, unless clumsy authorial explanations are offered.

Another sound effect that stands out is the jungle-like cries that accompany the lurid menacing shadows on the walls in Scenes 10 and 11. These inhuman noises represent the confusion and terror in Blanche's mind and, like the polka, are only heard by her, though they also serve to create a dramatic effect on stage.

Perhaps the use of music (and other sound effects) is again a technique learnt from the cinema. Williams uses sound effectively to focus our attention on Blanche's mental state. Naturally, descriptions on the printed page do not have the same impact as a stage performance. The readers of the play of course have to use their imagination – as the director of a play does in the early stages of work. Again, the drama acted out in the reader's mind cannot equal the force of the play on stage, though it may capture in nuances of mood what it lacks in definition.

## FOCUS

Though far from being the heroine of classical tragedy, Blanche still commands our attention. After her arrival in Elysian Fields she is hardly ever off the stage; even offstage, she is heard singing, taking one of her long baths. In Scene 7 she is happily singing sentimental popular songs in contrapuntal contrast to the lurid revelations of her past being told by Stanley in the kitchen. The same technique is used in the last scene, where Blanche's fussy instructions about her outfit provide an ironic background to her sister's conversation with Eunice about the arrangements for Blanche's committal to a mental hospital.

On stage or offstage, Blanche remains the centre of attention. If you glance through the play, you will find that every scene (except perhaps Scene 4) ends with Blanche centre stage, commanding our attention with an arresting phrase or a dramatic gesture.

In the last scene particularly, this pathetic, deluded woman assumes the dignity she has been lacking. Her irritating mannerisms, so amply displayed earlier in this scene, seem to fall away, and she leaves on the doctor's arm without a backward glance, speaking her famous line: 'Whoever you are – I have always depended on the kindness of strangers' (p. 89). Though the very last words of the play, spoken by Steve, refer to the poker game, yet they too serve to underline the **pathos** of Blanche's fate, by the very unconcern they show.

Blanche stands isolated by her ignorance of her future, and by the behaviour of those around her. The pathos of her ignorance has the effect of diminishing those who are deceiving her: the hysterical Stella; the blustering bully Stanley. The change in her status is demonstrated by the players standing up awkwardly as she passes through. This gesture of courtesy contrasts with Stanley's 'Nobody's going to get up' (p. 26) in Scene 3, and makes the point very clearly – but on both occasions the focus is on Blanche.

Earlier, the conventions of Greek tragedy (see commentary on **Scene 11** in **The Text**), which demand the downfall of a noble hero as result of his pride, were contrasted with Williams' elevation of a vain, self-deluded, promiscuous woman to the stature of a heroine. The focus of audience attention throughout, Blanche rises above her degradation and inspires in the audience the pity and fear demanded by classical tragedy. In the end, like the card players, we too salute her.

**QUESTION**

Is the contrapuntal effect of Blanche's singing offstage intended to stress the irony of the situation or to arouse our pity for her?

## LANGUAGE AND STYLE

Two levels of language are used in *A Streetcar Named Desire* – the words spoken by the characters in the play and the text of the stage directions.

The words spoken by the characters in a play matter greatly, and not only for conveying their thoughts and emotions. The way they speak helps us to form an opinion of their natures, to decide whether we like or dislike them, and helps us to understand their motives in acting as they do. Moreover, the nuances of speech set the characters in their class context and show the differences of social status and education as well as of emotional and intellectual make-up – these aspects too will affect their actions in the play. In *A Streetcar Named Desire* the very marked differences between Stanley and Blanche are stressed as much by Stanley's non-grammatical, slangy, often carelessly slurred speech as by Blanche's high-flown rhetoric which often rings false (as it is meant to, revealing her pretensions) and never lets us forget that she was a teacher of English. At times there is a lyrical quality in her words, emphasising their emotional content.

Stella too speaks correct English, but in a matter-of-fact, mostly unemotional tone. However, when she speaks of her love for her husband, she betrays the intensity of her passion.

Eunice and Steve are firmly set a rung or two below Stanley on the class ladder, as much by the way they speak as by their drunken public quarrels.

Mitch too is defined by the way he speaks: his efforts at speaking properly are marred by his genteel circumlocutions – 'I perspire' (Scene 6, p. 52), never 'I sweat' – as much as by his grammatical slip-ups: 'he don't look' (Scene 6, p. 54); 'We was' (Scene 6, p. 53). He cannot follow or match Blanche's flights of fancy – her whimsy about the Pleiades in Scene 6 is a prime example – and is acutely aware of this.

As we have seen, the way the characters in a play speak is the most important indicator of their natures, their social status and their emotional make-up. Try to imagine forming an idea of the people in this play from their actions alone. The result would be flat, almost incomprehensible, unless the actors adopted the exaggerated gestures of mime.

Only the characters' speech gives them life, and it is a measure of the dramatist's art that he can turn characters into credible human beings by what they say and how they say it. The words he chooses to put into their mouths and the way he makes them speak are all-important.

There is, of course, another kind of language to be found in the play: the stage directions. Williams' stage directions are unusually detailed (see **Visual and sound effects** in **Dramatic techniques** and **Characterisation**), ensuring that the sets evoke the right atmosphere. However, they are also remarkable for another reason: they are beautifully written, evocative, accurate, and employ poetic images to convey their meaning. In this respect they are quite unusual, and an added bonus for the reader of the play as against the spectator.

**CHECK
THE BOOK**
The stage directions in Shaw's *Saint Joan* are much longer than those of *A Streetcar*, much more detailed and prosaic, yet no more successful in achieving their aim of evoking a clear picture. Why could this be so?

# IMAGERY AND SYMBOLISM

In *A Dictionary of Literary Terms* by Martin Gray (Longman, 1984) imagery is defined as 'the figurative language in a piece of literature', that is, words referring to objects or qualities, which have the power to appeal directly to the senses and emotions of the reader, in order to convey thoughts and feelings in a more direct, as well as aesthetically satisfying, way. Metaphors and similes are the typical stock-in-trade of **figurative language**, though of course many other **tropes** are also employed.

**Symbolism,** on the other hand, is the use of something to represent a quality or a concept on the basis of some similarity between the symbol and the thing it represents. For instance, a peacock may represent vanity; or a lion, strength. These two examples may be described as conventional symbols, readily understood by everyone.

Writers often use symbols that are not so easily understood because they are based on private experience, on a personal vision of the world and life. Precisely because such symbols are not readily understood, and require either some knowledge of the writer's life or an intuitive empathy with the thinking behind the symbol, they are much more challenging and intriguing to the reader.

**QUESTION**

Is the use of figurative language in stage directions quite common? Can you think of another play that employs poetic language in the stage directions alone?

In *A Streetcar Named Desire* the imagery of the stage directions will attract the readers' attention. It is to be expected that Williams should make use of the evocative power of figurative language when he is trying to paint a word picture or convey in words the quality of a sound, and to do so in as few words as possible, in order to fit his description into the conventional length of stage directions. Thus in Scene 1 the phrase *'the infatuated fluency of brown fingers'* (p. 3) conveys the black pianist's skilful playing, their total absorption in the music, and their pleasure in it.

In Scene 11 the Varsouviana polka is *'filtered into weird distortion'* (p. 87) in Blanche's mind. The harsh discords that seem to caricature the dance tune are a signal that the sad memories of the past are about to give way to the harsh reality of her institutionalised future.

The use of imagery is not limited to Tennessee Williams' stage directions, however. As befits a teacher of English and a poetry-lover, Blanche frequently uses figurative language when she is emotionally moved. In Scene 5 she says she has to 'put on soft colours, the colours of butterfly wings, and glow' (p. 45); in Scene 6 she describes love as being like 'a blinding light on something that had always been half in shadow' (p. 56); and in Scene 9 she speaks of the paddy-wagon picking up drunken soldiers 'like daisies' (p. 74), an unexpectedly humorous image.

While such figurative language may be expected from Blanche, surprisingly we also find Stanley using metaphors when he is moved. He employs the startling and evocative phrase 'coloured lights' twice in Scene 8 to describe the ecstasy of passion; and when he is brutally destroying Blanche's illusions in Scene 10, he describes her evening gown and tiara as 'that worn-out Mardi Gras outfit, rented for fifty cents from some rag-picker' (p. 79). His use of such images is all the more memorable for being so entirely unexpected.

When it comes to symbolism, the first symbol to strike the reader is of course to be found in the title of the play, a streetcar bound for Desire (and then for Cemeteries). The streetcar stands not only for Blanche's headlong descent into disaster, but also for Tennessee Williams' lifelong pursuit of sexual partners. (See **Desire and Fate** in **Themes** for a discussion of this and other symbols. It was to be expected that a writer like Tennessee Williams should express his private terrors in symbols.) The very same symbol of the streetcar is used by both sisters in Scene 4 as a euphemism for sexual experience. In Scenes 4, 6 and 10, the headlong rush of a locomotive is another symbol of relentless Fate, though perhaps used less consistently and less successfully.

Like the streetcar's destination, Desire, the stop called Elysian Fields is an obvious symbol. It is used ironically, however, as the Elysian Fields – the abode of the blessed dead in Greek mythology – turn out to be a rundown street in New Orleans.

The spilt coke on Blanche's skirt in Scene 5 is another symbol, recalling perhaps the blood spilt by her husband's suicide (or perhaps Blanche's 'stained' reputation). Of course, her endless baths stand for her desire to be cleansed of her guilt for her husband's death and of her promiscuous past.

The Chinese paper lantern hiding the naked light bulb is a symbol of Blanche's longing for what she calls 'magic' (Scene 9, p. 72), the dressing up of ugly reality. When first Mitch (Scene 9) and then Stanley (Scene 11) tear it off, she cries out as if in pain. The light of the lantern also brings to mind the moth attracted to light, an image used of Blanche's fragility (Scene 1).

It is noticeable that most of these symbols concern Blanche. This is understandable – after all she is the focus of this play, the character with which Tennessee Williams identified most, and, moreover, one whose great need was to find another, more bearable, reality in her imagination.

As well as symbols expressed in visual images or in words, Williams rather unusually uses music to convey a message. The blue piano

> **CONTEXT**
>
> Ritual cleansing has a long history, going back to Pontius Pilate who 'took water and washed his hands' after the Jews had demanded the death of Jesus (Matthew 26:24).

stands for the callous vitality of the Vieux Carré of New Orleans, while the Varsouviana polka recalls the tragedy in Blanche's past.

**QUESTION**

Do you find the use of the polka consistent in the message it conveys, especially in Scene 11?

The significance of both musical themes goes beyond merely providing a touch of local colour. They mark a change of mood, convey a menace, and underline a tragic development. The blue piano in particular can signal a variety of messages whereas the polka is specifically linked with the suicide of Blanche's husband and is heard by her, and by her alone, when she remembers him. The only exception to this occurs in Scene 11, when the polka is heard as Blanche emerges from the bathroom, again as the doctor and nurse ring the bell, and finally distorted into inhuman jungle cries that signal the threat of human cruelty. Significantly, they die out as Blanche listens to the doctor's gentle, courteous voice.

Both these musical symbols will, of course, be appreciated more keenly by the theatre audience, though perhaps not all of the spectators will realise that Blanche alone can hear the polka. Certainly in this respect the readers of the play are at a disadvantage, as stage directions can never have the same dramatic impact as the music starting up on the stage.

On another level Stanley and Blanche may be regarded as symbols of the two Americas: the decadent old plantation culture rooted in the slavery system; and the new America of the immigrants – urban, egalitarian, ruthless, vibrantly alive.

All these symbols are used deliberately. A dramatist will naturally think in images to express the emotions that inspired the play. It is the reader's (or spectator's) exciting task to identify the symbols and try to interpret them. Most of Williams' symbols are easy to understand – and are no less effective dramatically for that. Symbolic language in a play has to be readily understood by the audience who will not have the leisure to consider hidden meanings while the action moves forward.

Of course, the readers of the play have the time to look for other symbols, less obvious ones perhaps: Stella's reading a comic (Scene 4);

and the baby's pale blue blanket (Scene 11), which tells us that Stanley's luck is in and that he has the son he wanted.

# MORALITY PLAY OR MELODRAMA?

## MORALITY PLAY?

At first glance, the question posed by the title of this section may seem inappropriate. A play about drinking, violence, promiscuity and betrayal can hardly be described as 'moral', and certainly there are no lines in the play warning us against sin.

The very title of the play, with its image of a streetcar running unnervingly along its tracks, driven by desire, seems to imply that those who board this car are helpless once they have made their choice to ride in it. Though the ultimate fate of the play's characters is not revealed, we will remember that in Scene 1 Blanche changes from the streetcar to Desire, to one going to Cemeteries. Desire and Cemeteries, sin and death – the message is clear.

The conversation between the two sisters in Scene 4 is quite explicit about the 'brutal desire' (p. 40) that decides their choice. Blanche goes further in her bitter words that the rickety streetcar of desire brought her to where she is now, destitute and living on her sister's charity. Behind these words there is both self-knowledge and self-condemnation.

Ominously the sober, matter-of-fact Stella offers no words of self-criticism before the last scene, when for a short time she confronts her guilt: 'Oh, God, what have I done to my sister?' (p. 88). Moments later, in the middle of her *'luxurious'* sobbing, she yields to Stanley's lovemaking, compounding her guilt.

Though there is no admission of sin or guilt in the play, yet we are aware that, inexorably, there is a downward movement towards catastrophe, and that some measure of punishment will be meted out to the guilty. Blanche, stripped of her fanciful illusions, goes to the mental hospital; Stella will continue in her passionate involvement with her husband but her betrayal of her sister will

**CONTEXT**

The image of the streetcar as the driving force of passion conveys the helplessness of its riders, but stresses also the element of choice; they have chosen to board the streetcar. The implied moral message is clear.

stay with her; Stanley may bluster as before, but even if he can put out of his mind what he has done, his wife and his loyal admirers will surely look askance at him sometimes, wonder and condemn him. The punishment may not be death but it will be the bitter taste of guilt.

For years it was not in Williams' nature to make an open confession of his homosexuality and promiscuity. It seems, however, that he found ways, open or oblique, of speaking of them in his plays. The morality of his stance, seemingly hypocritical, is expressed in the fate he deals out to those who transgress.

## MELODRAMA?

Melodrama was originally a play with music (hence its name), but later the term came to be used of naively sensational plays featuring horrible murders, ghosts and dramatic villainies. Nowadays we think of melodrama as a play with plenty of violent action, with murders and wicked plots, with main characters of either exaggerated virtue or deepest wickedness.

An essential ingredient of a melodrama is the sensational character of both the plot and the actions of the characters. If we consider the leading characters of *A Streetcar Named Desire* – the promiscuous, deluded Blanche; her sister, married to a violent primitive man of a class well below her own; the husband who determines to rid himself of the welcome visitor – we find all the ingredients of a melodrama.

As we read through the play we come upon plenty of melodramatic incidents: Stanley rifling though Blanche's finery (Scene 2); his drunken rage (Scene 3); Blanche's hysteria (Scenes 3 and 4); Blanche's revelation of her husband's suicide and its causes (Scene 6); Stanley 'clearing the table' (Scene 8); Mitch's attempted rape of Blanche (Scene 9); and Stanley raping Blanche (Scene 10). Evidently there are more than enough incidents in the play to justify calling it a melodrama.

And yet if we consider the play as a whole, these incidents are not there to thrill the audience (as in a melodrama). They are introduced

to throw a light on the characters and their motives, to explain complex emotions below the surface. Also, it might be said that any dramatist worth his salt will introduce a hint of melodrama into his/her plays to raise and maintain dramatic tension. Moreover, the subtle and variable language of *A Streetcar* is not to be found in a melodrama.

*A Streetcar Named Desire* may have been a *succès de scandale* when it was first staged (see **Critical history**), but now we see it as a sombre, serious drama.

> **CONTEXT**
>
> We do not need to look far for melodramatic aspects of other plays – think of Shakespeare's *Hamlet*.

## PART FOUR

## CRITICAL HISTORY

# EARLY RECEPTION

*A Streetcar Named Desire* was written and staged in the 1940s, a period when the American cinema was at the height of its popularity, and theatre audiences were deeply influenced – one might say conditioned – by the movies.

Williams' *A Streetcar Named Desire* was a mixture of sex, violence and morality (this last, however, present only implicitly), a recipe tested out successfully in the cinema. The play drew also on the romantic myth of the American South, as did Williams' first really successful play *The Glass Menagerie.* This myth was reinforced by the fantastic success of MGM's *Gone with the Wind* (1939), starring Vivien Leigh. Though Williams did not accept the romanticised view of the South uncritically, he undoubtedly made use of it in the tragic figure of Blanche Dubois.

The much-praised staging of *The Glass Menagerie* (premiered in Chicago in 1944 and transferred in 1945 to New York where it ran for 561 performances) obviously raised the expectations of both the theatre critics and the audiences for Williams' follow-up play. There was a readiness in the audience to accept a play that departed considerably from the accepted formula of the traditional 'well-made play' and used unexpected, non-realistic methods to stress what the playwright regarded as the play's significant scenes and values.

The way had been prepared for Williams by Thornton Wilder (1897–1975) in his plays *Our Town* (1938) and *The Skin of Our Teeth* (1942). In the former play the conventional storyline fades into insignificance as the living and dead of a small American town mingle on the stage. *The Skin of Our Teeth* presents the Antrobus family living simultaneously in the Stone Age and through the ages up to present-day America.

 **CHECK THE BOOK**

Williams makes the point about such innovations in his preface to *The Glass Menagerie,* where he explains his 'unconventional techniques' of using screen images and titles in the play, and his 'conception of a new, plastic theatre' so that the theatre would 'resume vitality as part of our culture'.

In *The Glass Menagerie* Williams uses the projection of screen images and titles, and introduces a recurrent tune, 'The Glass Menagerie'. Though he abandoned the use of screen images in the acting version of the play, his intention to use them is significant, and makes understandable his use of **Expressionist** evil shapes and jungle-like cries, as well as of the blue piano and Varsouviana polka in *A Streetcar Named Desire*.

Another, quite different type of new drama emerged in the late forties and the fifties. Concerned primarily with social and moral issues, as represented in the work of Arthur Miller (b. 1915), it remained outside Williams' sphere of interest. Yet it was Miller who paid his 'Memorial Tribute to Tennessee Williams' in a speech to the American Academy in 1984, shrewdly identifying Williams' 'rhapsodic insistence on making form serve his utterance. He did not turn his back on dramatic rules but created new ones'.

After tryouts in Boston, New Haven and Philadelphia, *A Streetcar Named Desire* opened in New York on 3 December 1947. The reception was very favourable. Richard Watts Jnr in the *New York Post* of 4 December 1947 hailed its author as 'an oncoming playwright of power, imagination and an almost desperately morbid turn of mind and emotion', while Louis Kronberger in *PM* of 5 December 1947 described *A Streetcar* as 'an enormous advance over that minor-key and too wet-eyed work, *The Glass Menagerie*'. There was a glowing review by the doyen of New York critics, Brooks Atkinson, in the *New York Times* on 4 December 1947, in which he also pointed out that Williams presented the theatre with considerable problems because of his avoidance of conventional form. Indeed, some reviewers criticised the episodic nature of the play, failing to recognise its significance for the theatre of the future. In the *New York Herald Tribune* of 4 December 1947 Howard Barnes praised Tennessee Williams as 'the Eugene O'Neill of the present period'. Harold Clurman in *Tomorrow*, February 1948, stressed the impact of *A Streetcar Named Desire* as 'especially strong because it is virtually unique as a stage piece that is both personal and social'.

There were also some less complimentary reviews, notably by Ward Morehouse in the *Sun*, 4 December 1947, in which *A Streetcar* was

**CONTEXT**

Eugene O'Neill (1888–1956), to whom Williams was compared, was an internationally renowned American dramatist, who enjoyed success in the Thirties. His most famous play is probably *The Iceman Cometh* (published 1939, staged 1946).

described as 'not a play for the squeamish', recalling the phrase 'an almost desperately morbid turn of mind' in the otherwise favourable review by Richard Watts Jnr mentioned above.

*Time* of 15 December 1947 declared that 'the play could stand more discipline … There is sometimes an absence of form. And it could stand more variety; only the clash between Blanche and Stanley gets real emotion and drama into the play'. *Time* went on giving negative notices to Williams' plays until 1962, when it suddenly called him 'the greatest living playwright anywhere'.

It should be mentioned here that *A Streetcar Named Desire* was the first play to win three major awards: the Pullitzer, the Donaldson and the New York Dramatic Critics' Circle awards. It ran in New York for 855 performances.

As some of the reviews make clear, *A Streetcar* was to some extent a *succès de scandale*, dealing with sex to an extent, and in a manner not encountered on the stage up till then. We may observe, however, that sex was still a subject not to be discussed on stage too openly. Thus in Scene 4 the two sisters talking bout sex use the metaphor of a streetcar with the name of Desire instead. In Scene 7 Stella refers to 'things about [her] sister …that caused sorrow at home' (p. 61) while in Scene 9 Blanche speaks of her 'many intimacies with strangers' (p. 73). Understandably perhaps, the rape is never spoken of as such in the last scene of the play.

What was new in *A Streetcar* was the combination of realism and lyricism. To some extent this was the obvious result of presenting in the same play a character like Blanche who lives in a dream world and uses the language of a schoolteacher and a poetry-lover, and characters like Stanley and Steve, uneducated men whose world is circumscribed by drinking, card-playing and chasing women. Yet this is not simply a matter of pitting an educated speaker against an uneducated one.

The psychology of the characters is realistic, their motives and action seem wholly credible, taken scene by scene, but as the action moves inexorably to the climax of Scene 10 it rises above everyday reality into the realm of high tragedy. Mirroring the change in the

**CONTEXT**

The realism of the setting (a shabby apartment in a run-down house) and of the characters (factory workers and a schoolteacher out of a job) contrasts with the unexpected feasts of lyricism in the dialogue and the high drama of the last three scenes.

characters and the action, the setting too, entirely realistic at first – a two-room apartment with a bathroom in a shabby house in New Orleans – undergoes a change. The walls dissolve, lurid shapes appear and jungle noises are heard.

As the characters and the setting change, they appear less predictable and their unexpected ambiguity heightens the dramatic tension. The dramatic potential of unpredictability, the essential mystery of human nature are exploited here as they will be in a much more sensational form in Williams' later plays. Yet the sensationalism that was often seized upon by the critics is in the end not what characterises Williams' work. What the audience senses is the terrifying mystery, the changeability of human nature, the unpredictability of fate.

In England *A Streetcar Named Desire* was mostly well received after its British premiere on 12 October 1949, under the direction of Laurence Olivier, with Vivien Leigh as Blanche, Bonar Colleano as Stanley, Renee Asherson as Stella and Bernard Braden as Mitch. There were glowing reviews in the *Daily Express* and the *Evening Standard* and in the quality weeklies (for instance R. D. Smith's review in the *New Statesman & Nation* on 22 October 1949). Harold Hobson in the Sunday Times of 13 November 1949 described it as 'strictly and even puritanically' a valuable play.

The reviews seemed to focus on the sexual aspect of the play. Thus J. C. Trewin in the *Illustrated London News* dismissed *A Streetcar* as 'a squalid anecdote of a nymphomaniac's decay in a New Orleans slum'. Such condemnations are particularly noteworthy when we remember that they came after the cuts in the text which the Lord Chamberlain had insisted on.

 **QUESTION**

Is J. C. Trewin's dismissal of the play as 'a squalid anecdote' fair? Which aspects of the play does Trewin ignore?

Questions were asked in Parliament about the misuse of public funds in financing such an immoral play – a reference to an Arts Council grant towards the London production of the play. Still the play ran for a respectable total of 326 performances.

In France, an adaptation of *A Streetcar Named Desire* opened in Paris as *Un Tramway Nommé Désir*, an adaptation by Jean Cocteau

**CONTEXT**

Jean Cocteau
(1889–1963) was a
French poet,
dramatist and film
director. His
phenomenal early
success with a
volume of poetry
at the age of
twenty continued
throughout his
life. His novels
include *Les
enfants terribles*
(1929), and his
best-known films
are *La Belle et la
bête* (1945) and *Le
Testament
d'Orphée* (1960).

with Arletty as Blanche. Perhaps surprisingly, in view of the popular idea of French morality, many disapproving voices were heard, and not just from the gallery. The reviews, on the whole, were rather less favourable than might have been expected. Thus André Alter in *L'Aube* of 20 October 1949 spoke of the frightening emptiness, shallowness of the play, which even Lila de Nobili's designs failed to fill. Jean-Jacques Gautier in the *Figaro* of 19 October 1949 described the play as 'filled with undressing, morbid events, fights and games … obscenities and murders'. The Cocteau version ran for 233 performances.

## LATER REVIVALS

Though seen by many as sensationalist to begin with, over the years *A Streetcar Named Desire* came to be regarded as an American classic, almost a part of American popular culture. Stanley's drunken bellow of 'Stell-lahhhh' and Blanche's poignant last words in the play 'I have always depended on the kindness of strangers' (p. 89) were remembered and quoted.

Not surprisingly, in the United States the play has been revived twelve times since its first staging in New York in 1947, for the last time (at the time of going to press) in 1992. The revivals attracted attention, though not always praise. The most notable among them was the 1949–50 Road Company production with Uta Hagen and Anthony Quinn. In 1956 came the New York staging with Tallulah Bankhead and Gerald O'Laughlin. There were also innovative multi-racial and all-black productions in 1953, 1956 and 1958.

In 1973 a revival in Los Angeles was directed by James Bridges, with Faye Dunaway as Blanche and Jon Voight as Stanley. Stephen Faber in the *New York Times* of 1 April 1973 cruelly dismissed Voight's performance: 'Voight's studious attempt to underplay the role is disastrous. His relatively quiet, halting ineffectual Stanley makes little sense on any level. He even throws dishes politely. Voight simply has no menace; he never believes he has the power to destroy Blanche'.

Also in 1973 came another New York revival at the Lincoln Center, with Rosemary Harris and James Farentino in the leading roles. In 1988 another production was staged in New York under the direction of Alex Baldwin, with Blythe Danner as Blanche and Aiden Quinn as Stanley. Edith Oliver's review in the *New Yorker*, March 1988, was interesting, though not particularly complimentary: Quinn's Stanley was seen by her as 'too much a man of the eighties to make sex seem menacing'.

The last major revival was in 1992, again in New York, under the direction of Gregory Moshed, with Jessica Lange and Alex Baldwin. The play was also presented on ABC Television on 4 March 1984, with Ann-Margret and Treat Williams, and in CBS 'Playhouse 90' on 29 October 1995, with Jessica Lange and Alex Baldwin.

The London audience had to wait until 1974 for the first major revival of the play, directed by Edwin Sherwin, with Claire Bloom as Blanche and Martin Shaw as Stanley. Jack Tinker in the *Daily Mail* of 11 March 1974 had nothing but praise for Claire Bloom: 'Until now [Blanche's] steamy legend has belonged exclusively to Vivien Leigh. However, legends are only ever on loan and Bloom is here in London to prove how much mileage is left in the old *Streetcar*.' Similarly, Eric Johns in *Stage and Television Today* of 14 March 1974 declared 'No ghost will haunt Claire Bloom's Blanche'. John Walker in the *International Herald Tribune* of 23–4 March 1974 spoke of Bloom's Blanche as having 'all of Blanche's bitterness as well as vulnerability'.

The most recent revival (at the time of going to press) was in 2002 at the National Theatre under the direction of Trevor Nunn, with Glenn Close as Blanche and Iain Glen as Stanley. The reviews were somewhat mixed; not surprisingly, in this age of the cult of celebrity, they concentrated on Glenn Close. Benedict Nightingale in *The Times* of 9 October 2002 spoke of 'a Blanche who … has moments of surprising radiance, wry insight, defensive rage … and a wincing, palpitating desperation'. Sheridan Morley in the *New Statesman* of 21 October 2002 remarked that 'Close [is] about as vulnerable as a Sherman tank' in 'this production which aches to be a musical'. Georgina Brown in the *Mail on Sunday* of 13 October 2002 saw

**QUESTION**

Do you think that present day theatre audiences will judge *A Streetcar* differently because of the rise of feminism?

**QUESTION**

Is Blanche a 'melodramatic character' in a realistic play?

Close's Blanche as 'not a threat … but an irritation, the thick-skinned sister-in-law from hell who hogs the bathroom'. In a more serious vein, for John Peter in the *Sunday Times* of 13 October 2002, Close's Blanche is a performer: 'Life is a succession of glamorous tableaux in which Blanche is the glamorous but anguished central figure … Close brings out … the difference between a melodramatic actress and a melodramatic character.'

What may well surprise us is the change of emphasis in the conception of both the central characters. Stanley seems to be losing the machismo of the '*gaudy seed-bearer*' (Scene 1, p. 14), the bullying pride. Blanche, on the other hand, has grown in assertiveness. Claire Bloom's performance of 1974 stresses the bitterness in Blanche, as well as her vulnerability. When it comes to the 2002 revival, the choice of Glenn Close as Blanche speaks for itself. Close, the vengeful 'bunny boiler' of the film *Fatal Attraction* is hardly Tennessee Williams' fluttering 'moth', though she won praise for her performance from some reviewers at least. Whether the introduction of third-millennium sexual politics into a play so firmly rooted in its period is justified, remains a question to ponder.

## PART FIVE

## BACKGROUND

# TENNESSEE WILLIAMS

Thomas Lanier Williams was born on 26 March 1911 in Columbus, Mississippi (the nickname 'Tennessee' was given to him later at college by a fellow student ignorant of the geography of the Southern states, who confused Mississippi – where Williams was born – with Tennessee). His father, Cornelius Coffin Williams, was then an employee of a telephone company, and his mother Edwina, a typical spoilt, impractical Southern belle, was the daughter of a highly respected Episcopalian rector, the Rev. Walter E. Dakin.

There were three children born to the marriage, Thomas, or Tom, Rose, two years younger, and Dakin, born eight years after Tom. The Williams marriage was not happy, and Mrs Williams turned more and more to the children and to the comfort of her parents' rectory. She enjoyed sharing her parents' position of esteem in a small town until her husband took up the post of manager in a shoe company in St Louis, and the family moved there in 1919.

The move was disastrous both for the children, who missed their grandparents' house, and for their mother who suddenly became a nonentity in a large city, losing her established status in Columbus. As the relations between husband and wife worsened Cornelius Williams started to drink heavily. At this time also Rose's behaviour began to cause concern. Tom suffered much from the unhappiness at home and found consolation in reading and later in writing.

In 1928 came a temporary respite when Tom was invited to accompany his grandfather, the Rev. Dakin, and a group of his parishioners on a trip to Europe. The liberating effect of this trip remained with Tom, and he returned to Europe regularly throughout his life.

In 1929 his grandparents' generosity enabled Tom to become a student at the University of Missouri, at Columbia. Not

> **CONTEXT**
> The parallels with Williams' play *The Glass Menagerie* are quite startling.

**CHECK THE BOOK**
These dramatists are worth reading, even if only selectively (see **Further reading**).

distinguished academically, he nevertheless profited greatly by his three years there. He read voraciously (in particular the modern European dramatists – Anton Chekhov, August Strindberg, Henrik Ibsen) and began to make a name for himself as a writer.

The Depression put an end to his studies, and in 1931 he became a clerk in the shoe firm employing his father. This was a miserable time for Tennessee Williams, and he suffered a nervous breakdown. When his family's finances improved, he became a student at the Washington University in St Louis. He wrote a handful of plays, put on by small amateur companies.

An unhappy time followed, when his sister Rose became quite mentally unstable, and accused her father of attacking her. The sexual element in her fancies spelt scandal and so alarmed her mother that she agreed to a pre-frontal lobotomy to be performed on her daughter in 1937. Tennessee Williams was away at the State University of Iowa at this time, and he never ceased to reproach himself for not having been there to prevent the operation. Nor could he ever forgive his mother for her part in the business. This harrowing time left its mark on Tennessee Williams, and on his work: *The Glass Menagerie* is obviously autobiographical, and there is much of Rose in the unstable Blanche of *A Streetcar Named Desire*.

There followed a period of drifting for Tennessee Williams, which took him also to New Orleans. It seems that there he discovered his sexual identity and became a practising homosexual. Sexual liberation went hand in hand with confidence in his work. A collection of three short plays, *American Blues*, won a prize in 1939, and Audrey Wood, head of the best theatrical agency, took him up the following year. She succeeded in obtaining for him a Rockefeller fellowship in the same year, and he was awarded another, smaller Rockefeller scholarship too.

Audrey Wood obtained for Williams a contract as scriptwriter with MGM in 1943. Though his only script, *The Gentleman Caller*, was turned down by MGM, it became the basis of his first successful play, *The Glass Menagerie*. Moreover, scriptwriting certainly influenced the technique of his plays (see **Structure** in **Dramatic techniques**).

The successful staging of *A Glass Menagerie* in New York in 1945 spurred Tennessee Williams on to his next major play, *A Streetcar Named Desire*. The writing of the play gave him some trouble, as witness the change of title (and of emphasis) from 'The Moth' to 'Blanche's Chair in the Moon' to 'The Poker Night' before finally, after his move to New Orleans, to *A Streetcar Named Desire*.

The play opened in 1947 and was a great success. Tennessee Williams was by now a wealthy man, having sold the screen rights for both the plays, and deriving a good income from the stage productions as well.

The pattern of his life was now set for some time – visits to Europe, writing: a novel, *The Roman Spring of Mrs Stone* (1950); another film script, this time successful, *Baby Doll* (1951); several successful plays, *The Rose Tattoo* (1951), *Casino Real* (1953), *Cat on a Hot Tin Roof* (1955), *Orpheus Descending* (1957), *Suddenly Last Summer* (1958), *Sweet Bird of Youth* (1959), *Period of Adjustment* (1960), and *The Night of the Iguana* (1961).

**CHECK THE FILM**
The titles of most of his works will be quite familiar to filmgoers.

Success did not seem to bring him happiness, though. He underwent psychotherapy for depression; his drug-taking and drinking increased, as did his frenetic search for sexual encounters, which caused much pain to his live-in partner for many years, Frank Merlo.

Tennessee Williams' writing deteriorated. Though he wrote several plays between 1962 and his death, none of them was really successful. By now he was so befuddled by drink and drugs (after an unsuccessful drastic treatment in a mental hospital to which he had been committed by his brother) that he seemed quite indifferent to his failures.

He died in New York on 24 February 1983 in a hotel named the Elysée (an ironically appropriate name that recalls the Elysian Fields in *A Streetcar Named Desire*). He choked to death on one of his barbiturates.

## OTHER WORKS

**QUESTION**

'I must find characters who correspond to my own tensions' – is this a strength or a weakness in a dramatist?

As is usually the case with writers who rely heavily on their own life stories for inspiration, Tennessee Williams was always looking for subjects with which he could identify. It was a limitation, but also the source of the strength and vividness of his writing. As he himself put it, 'Frankly there must be some limitations in me as a dramatist … I must find characters who correspond to my own tensions' (quoted in *Tennessee Williams: Rebellious Puritan* by Nancy Tischler, p. 246). This being the case, it is not surprising that his first successful full-length play, *The Glass Menagerie*, reflects the traumas of his own life quite closely, very obviously relying for inspiration on the members of his own family and their family history.

Since his plays have a common source, that of his own life, they inevitably share several themes. Firstly, and most famously, there is the streetcar of desire hurtling along to disaster. The urge to seek pleasure, however destructive, which drove Tennessee Williams, especially in his later years, is to be found in Blanche in *A Streetcar Named Desire*, of course, and also in the homosexual Sebastian in *Suddenly Last Summer*, and in a female guise once more in the ageing Princess Kosmonopolis in *Sweet Bird of Youth*.

Secondly, the guilt Tennessee Williams felt about his sister Rose's committal to a mental hospital is paralleled by Tom's remorse in *The Glass Menagerie*, and by Stella's anguish at the close of *A Streetcar Named Desire*. In *Suddenly Last Summer* Mrs Venable tries to protect her dead son's reputation by seeking to destroy Catherine's memory, and her mind, by a frontal lobotomy. The attempt fails, and Mrs Venable's only regret is that it should have done so. Unlike Tom and Stella she would have had no feelings of guilt about her action if she had succeeded. The motive and the outcome are different, but the fate of Williams' sister was clearly in his mind here as well.

The third characteristic of Williams' major plays is their Southern background. Williams' Southern-ness and his love of the South, not often openly declared, still imbue most of his work – either directly through the location and the leading characters, as in *Baby Doll*,

*Cat on a Hot Tin Roof, Suddenly Last Summer*, or indirectly through nostalgic memories, based on what the Williams children heard often from their mother. *The Glass Menagerie* and *A Streetcar Named Desire* offer examples of such indirect inspiration. In *The Glass Menagerie* Amanda's recollections of her youth evidently draw on Mrs Williams' highly romanticised memories. In *A Streetcar*, the dream-like vision of Belle Reve might have been coloured by Mrs Williams' reminiscences, but the sordid deaths witnessed by Blanche and the intrusion of drunken soldiers on the lawn are Williams' own contributions. They may be seen to represent Williams' reaction against his mother's idealisation of the Southern past.

There is an unusual example of 'cross-inspiration' in the suicide of Blanche's husband in *A Streetcar*. It echoes quite clearly the death in *The Glass Menagerie* of Amanda's beau Bates Cutrere, who was shot and killed in a quarrel. Even the location of both tragedies is the same, Moon Lake Casino.

> **CONTEXT**
>
> In her dreams of a death at sea, Blanche again avoids reality.

The fourth, less prominent theme is the fear of death, more specifically death from cancer, which haunted Williams for most of his life. (His beloved grandmother died of cancer in 1943.) Williams' own fears are mirrored by Big Daddy's terrors in *Cat on a Hot Tin Roof*. In contrast to all the sordid deaths Blanche has witnessed, in *A Streetcar Named Desire* death is welcomed like a bridegroom in Blanche's daydream of dying at sea, and being buried at sea 'in a clean white sack' (Scene 11, p. 85).

Finally a (sometimes hidden) theme that runs through much of Williams' work is homosexuality. In *A Streetcar Named Desire* it features openly in the homosexuality of Blanche's husband, and in a disguise through her many 'intimacies with strangers' (Scene 9, p. 73), which parallel Williams' own frenetic search for ever new partners. There are those who believe that the tragic figure of Blanche Dubois is a transsexual presentation of the promiscuity of Williams himself.

In *Suddenly Last Summer* Sebastian is murdered and partly cannibalised by the native beggarboys on whom he had preyed. In

*Cat on a Hot Tin Roof* Brick's unconfessed homosexuality is brought out into the open by his wife, with tragic results.

All the homosexual relationships in these plays end in disaster: was it Tennessee Williams' intention to placate morality? Or was it an expression of his dislike of his own sexual inclinations, spoken of by Christopher Isherwood (see also **Historical background**). In the title of her book on Williams, Nancy Tischler calls him 'Rebellious Puritan', but perhaps in his heart he accepted the puritan morality after all.

Though the autobiographical themes discussed above recur in his later plays, it is clear that Williams could and did reach beyond his own experiences. One characteristic of Williams' plays that endures is a sense of looming tragedy: the streetcar named Desire all too often changes direction to Cemeteries.

## HISTORICAL BACKGROUND

### The Second World War (1939–45)

Although Tennessee Williams was working on *A Streetcar Named Desire* at the end of the Second World War, and the play was first staged in 1947, only two years after the war, there is hardly any mention of the recent cataclysmic events in it – only Stanley's brief reference to the Salerno landings in Scene 11. Indeed, the political changes that followed the Second World War, which included the Cold War and the rise of the United States to a world power, seemed to pass Williams by. This omission is characteristic of all Williams' plays and seems to emphasise that the plays exist in their own world and time. The resulting claustrophobic quality contributes to the dramatic tension they all share.

### American Civil War (1861–5)

The events that did affect Williams, like most Southerners, were those of the American Civil War. In spite of the romantic aura that surrounds it, the primary concerns of the Civil War were basically economic. First, and best known, there was the issue of slavery.

CONTEXT

The author Mark Twain, himself for many years a Mississippi pilot, once said that in the South the Civil War 'is what A.D. is elsewhere, they date from it'.

Slavery was seen as an evil in the North, but the Southern states regarded it as essential for the tobacco and cotton industries on which their wealth was founded. When Abraham Lincoln was elected president in 1860, wanting to keep the union from breaking up, he promised the Southern states that slavery would continue to be legal in the states where it already existed. At first the Northern half of the United States wanted only to stop slavery spreading to other states but gradually, as the anti-slavery feeling grew stronger, total abolition of slavery became the declared aim of the North.

Another economic question that divided the South from the North was the demand of the American manufacturing industry, based largely in the North, for a tax on imported goods. The Southern states regarded this as an infringement of their rights and threatened to secede from the union.

There had been unrest among the slaves and the slave-owning states felt themselves to be more and more under threat. The break-up of the union became a reality as, one by one, seven Southern states (Georgia, Alabama, Florida, Mississippi, Louisiana, South Carolina and Texas) seceded, forming the Confederate States of America. After a Southern attack on Fort Sumter in South Carolina which was held by union (i.e. Northern) troops, President Lincoln denounced the Confederate states as rebels. Four more Southern states broke away (Virginia, North Carolina, Arkansas and Tennessee), and the war began.

The war ended with Confederate surrender in April 1865. By then, much of the South lay in ruins and though Lincoln hoped to 'bind up the South's wounds', he was assassinated a few days after the surrender, shot by an actor, John Wilkes Booth, a man with a deep hatred of the Union.

As a result, the treatment of the South was very harsh, and it took a long time for it to recover, especially when slavery was finally abolished a few years later. There is no doubt that the Southern defeat was exploited by Northerners moving in, which added to the bitterness of defeat. In economic decline, the South soon came to exercise an enduring influence on the imagination of writers in the South, and in the North as well.

> **CONTEXT**
>
> The Northerners moving in were nicknamed 'carpetbaggers' because they would arrive with only a carpetbag of personal belongings to further their political careers and make their fortunes.

## Homosexuality and the law

Uninterested in the Second World War, Williams seemed equally indifferent to a political issue that gained greatly in significance during his lifetime, and which might have been expected to have touched him closely: the question of gay rights. The politicising of what was basically a moral issue was successful in achieving its aims, and its impact on literature and the performing arts was great. Yet Williams appeared unmoved by the movement or by its success.

The issue of homosexuality, so prominent in his private life, is clearly a strand in his work, but never the central theme, and certainly never taken up to be defended or pleaded for. We must remember, of course, that for the greater part of Williams' life homosexuality was still illegal, though tolerated in some areas (New Orleans; Key West, Florida). This might explain his reluctance to give prominence to the issue.

According to Christopher Isherwood and others, however, there might have been another reason for Tennessee Williams' refusal to take up this cause. They maintain that he hated being a homosexual, and could not accept those who came to terms with their sexual orientation (see *The Kindness of Strangers: The Life of Tennessee Williams* by Donald Spoto, p. 320).

**QUESTION**

Do social issues figure prominently in Tennessee Williams' plays?

When accused of never dealing with homosexuality openly, Tennessee Williams declared in an interview with *Gay Sunshine* that the main thrust of his work was not sexual orientation but social issues: 'I am not about to limit myself to writing about gay people' (quoted in *The Kindness of Strangers: The Life of Tennessee Williams* by Donald Spoto, p. 319). The statement is open to doubt; homosexuality plays an important part in his plays, even when not openly discussed (see **Other works**, above), and he deals with social issues only in their most general sense of class snobbery, the resentment felt by people who see themselves as despised for their lack of social skills.

Though he seemed to disapprove, yet he felt compelled to introduce homosexuality into his plays (Blanche might equally have found her husband in bed with a woman, though of course the dramatic effect would have been less shocking). Also, in several of his plays we sense a condemnation of homosexuality (*A Streetcar Named Desire*, *Cat on a Hot Tin Roof*, *Suddenly Last Summer*).

A conflict existed then between his morality and his sexuality, never to be resolved, and never to be brought into the open in his plays, though the subject of gay rights was very much in the foreground of the political arena in the United States, especially during Williams' later years.

## LITERARY BACKGROUND

After the defeat of the Confederate army in 1865 the literature of the South revived gradually and began to thrive on the nostalgia for the past, on regional rather than national patriotism and on the romantic appeal of a lost cause and a lost way of life. A comparison might be made here with the romantic appeal of the defeated Royalists, the Cavaliers of seventeenth-century England, and of the Jacobite cause in Scotland.

The romanticising of the South went on into the twentieth century, and received a fresh impulse with Margaret Mitchell's famous 1936 novel *Gone with the Wind*, and especially with the phenomenal success of the 1939 film version of the novel.

Independent of this popular romantic image of the South, a new, separate, specifically Southern literature, The 'Mississippi School', emerged in the twentieth century. The fascination with the past merged gradually with an awareness of a South whose economic decay was symbolised by the decaying beauty of the planters' mansions (like Williams' Belle Reve).

Greed and treachery were recognised as part of the Southern character in the novels of William Faulkner, set in the imaginary Yoknapatawpha county, of Thomas Wolfe, Erskine Caldwell, and Williams' friend Carson McCullers.

**CHECK THE BOOK**

The subject of Rose Macaulay's 1932 novel is, as indicated by its title, *They Were Defeated*, the Royalist defeat in the Civil War. Sir Walter Scott's *Waverley* (1814) and *Redgauntlet* (1824), and R. L. Stevenson's *Kidnapped* (1886) and *Catriona* (1893) all have a Jacobite background.

**CHECK THE NET**

Consult the Internet Guide to Mississippi Writers on **http://olemiss.edu/mwp**.

One quality regarded as characteristic of the Southern writers was
their rich imagination, often bordering on the bizarre and the
grotesque – 'Southern Gothic' was the phrase used to describe it. Its
inspiration lay perhaps in an awareness of belonging to a dying
culture – dashing, romantic, but at the same time living on an
economy based on deep injustice and cruelty. The contradiction
inherent in the cultural climate favoured the individualistic, the
eccentric, and the outcast.

This was the Southern culture that appealed to Tennessee Williams.
His dislike of his mother had an adverse effect on his attitude to the
romanticised South, but the South as a broken, damaged society
with the ripe charms of decay, fired his imagination. As he himself
said, 'I write out of love for the South … once a way of life that I am
just old enough to remember – not a society based on money … I
write about the South because I think the war between romanticism
and the hostility to it is very sharp there' (quoted in *The Kindness of
Strangers: The Life of Tennessee Williams* by Donald Spoto, p. 139).
The South seemed to him to stand for cultural values ignored by the
money-grabbing, prosperous North of the carpetbaggers – thus
Blanche and Stanley may be seen as representing the two opposing
sides.

The subject matter of Williams' plays was deeply influenced by his
image of the South, but he looked to the playwrights of Europe for
models of the form. When a student at the University of Missouri,
and already dreaming of a career as a playwright, Tennessee
Williams immersed himself in the plays of Anton Chekhov, August
Strindberg and Henrik Ibsen. August Strindberg's *Miss Julie* (1888)
may well have influenced *A Streetcar Named Desire* in its equation
of class antagonism with sexual tension.

**CHECK
THE BOOK**

You will find no
sexual overtones,
however, in the
relationship
between Madame
Ranevska and
Lopakhin: Chekhov
certainly deals with
social issues.

Again, a parallel may be drawn between the plantation culture of
Belle Reve and the household of Madame Ranevska in Anton
Chekhov's *The Cherry Orchard* (1904). Both are doomed, useless,
living extravagantly on the labour of others, yet they both possess a
charm and romantic appeal lacking equally in the blustering
merchant Lopakhin in *The Cherry Orchard* and in Stanley
Kowalski.

As for Henrik Ibsen, Tennessee Williams could have wished for no better model for constructing a play round one compelling central character than *A Doll's House* (1879), *Hedda Gabler* (1890), *The Master Builder* (1892), or *John Gabriel Borkman* (1896), to name a few among many.

The two cultures – the Southern and the European – meet successfully in *A Streetcar Named Desire*.

> **CONTEXT**
>
> Seeing a performance of Ibsen's *Ghosts* in 1929 encouraged Williams to become a playwright.

| World events | 1939 | Arts | Tennessee Williams |
|---|---|---|---|
| Outbreak of Second World War in Europe | | Film version of Margaret Mitchell's *Gone with the Wind*, starring Clark Gable and Vivien Leigh<br><br>Film *The Wizard of Oz*, starring Judy Garland<br><br>Publication of the novel *The Grapes of Wrath* by John Steinbeck | *American Blues*, a collection of three short plays by Tennessee Williams wins a prize at the Group Theatre Play Contest |
| | **1940** | | |
| Battle of Britain | | *The Long Mirror* by J. B. Priestley is staged<br><br>Charlie Chaplin directs and stars in the film *The Great Dictator*<br><br>Publication of the novel *For Whom the Bell Tolls* by Ernest Hemingway | The play *Battle of Angels* is not a success |
| | **1941** | | |
| USA joins the Allies against the Axis powers in the Second World War | | Orson Welles directs and stars in the film *Citizen Kane*<br><br>Noel Coward's play *Blithe Spirit* is staged<br><br>The play *Long Day's Journey into Night* by Eugene O'Neill is written | |

| World events | | Arts | Tennessee Williams |
|---|---|---|---|
| | **1942** | | |
| US naval-air victory at Midway Island ends Japanese expansion in the Pacific | | Edward Hopper paints *Nighthawks*<br><br>Publication of the novel *L'Etranger* by Albert Camus | |
| | **1943** | | |
| British and American troops land at Salerno | | The Rodgers and Hammerstein musical *Oklahoma* is staged<br><br>Jean-Paul Sartre's essay *Being and Nothingness* is published | Obtains a contract as a scriptwriter for MGM |
| | **1944** | | |
| D-Day allied landings in Normandy | | Laurence Olivier directs and stars in the film *Henry V*<br><br>Bartok's Violin Concerto<br><br>Jean-Paul Sartre's play *Huis Clos* is staged | The play *The Glass Menagerie* is staged in Chicago |
| | **1945** | | |
| US President Franklin D. Roosevelt dies. He is succeeded by Harry S. Truman<br><br>American aircraft drops atomic bombs on Hiroshima and Nagasaki<br><br>End of Second World War | | The play *An Inspector Calls* by J. B. Priestley is staged<br><br>George Orwell's novel *Animal Farm* is published | Starts work on the play *A Streetcar Named Desire* |

| World events | 1946 | Arts | Tennessee Williams |
|---|---|---|---|
| An upsurge of labour unrest cripples large sections of US industry | | The play *The Iceman Cometh* by Eugene O'Neill is staged | |
| | | Publication of *A History of Western Philosophy* by Bertrand Russell | |
| | | Publication of the poetry collection *North and South* by Elizabeth Bishop | |
| India and Pakistan become independent | **1947** | Arthur Miller's play *All My Sons* is staged | *A Streetcar Named Desire* is staged |
| | | *The Linden Tree* by J. B. Priestley is staged | |
| | | Henri Cartier-Bresson holds one-man show at New York's Museum of Modern Art | |
| Britain, USA and France cooperate in establishing an airlift to West Berlin | **1948** | The play *The Browning Version* by Terence Rattigan is staged | |
| Gandhi assassinated in Delhi | | Swiss sculptor Alberto Giacometti has a successful exhibition in New York | |
| | | Laurence Olivier directs and stars in the film *Hamlet* | |
| | | The novel *La Peste* by Albert Camus is published | |

| World events | 1949 | Arts | Tennessee Williams |
|---|---|---|---|
| Chinese Communist People's Republic is proclaimed | | The essay *The Second Sex* by Simone de Beauvoir is published<br><br>Film *The Third Man* by Orson Welles is screened<br><br>Arthur Miller's play *Death of a Salesman* is staged | British premiere of *A Streetcar Named Desire* at the Aldwych Theatre, London, directed by Laurence Olivier |
| | **1950** | | |
| General MacArthur, commanding the UN forces, launches a counter-offensive against the North Korean invaders in the Korean War | | Commercial colour television broadcasting begins in the USA<br><br>Robert Doisneau produces the photograph *The Kiss* for *Life* magazine | *A Streetcar Named Desire* is staged in Paris, France<br><br>Publication of *The Roman Spring of Mrs Stone*, a novel |
| | **1951** | | |
| USA explodes the first hydrogen bomb | | The film *The African Queen*, starring Humphrey Bogart and Katharine Hepburn, is screened<br><br>The novel *The Catcher in the Rye* by J. D. Salinger is published | *A Streetcar Named Desire* is filmed, directed by Elia Kazan<br><br>*The Rose Tattoo* is staged |

## BIOGRAPHIES

A number of biographies of Tennessee Williams have been published, but most of them are of little interest except to those who are eager to learn more about his drug-taking and his homosexual affairs. There are, however, a few exceptions:

Ronald Hayman, *Tennessee Williams: Everyone Else is an Audience*, Yale University Press, New York and London, 1985
> A well-written biography with interesting quotations from Tennessee Williams and his friends

Donald Spoto, *The Kindness of Strangers: The Life of Tennessee Williams*, Bodley Head, 1985
> Crammed with facts yet surprisingly readable

Nancy M. Tischler, *Tennessee Williams: Rebellious Puritan*, The Citadel press, 1961
> A biography focusing on his work

Edwina Dakin Williams, *Remember Me to Tom*, G. P. Putnam's Sons, 1963; Cassell, 1964
> Mrs Williams' memories, ghosted by Lucy Freeman. Pedestrian in style but interesting, not least for what Mrs Williams has omitted to mention

Donald Windham, *Tennessee Williams' Letters to Donald Windham, 1940–65*, Holt, Rinehart & Winston, 1977
> Of literary as well as personal interest

## LITERARY CRITICISM

There have been few works of literary criticism of any depth on Tennessee Williams. Evidently his private life is deemed of more interest. A few works of literary criticism, mostly intended for students, are listed below:

Catherine M. Arnott, (compiler), *Tennessee Williams on File* (Writers on File Series), Methuen, 1985

Roger Boxill, *Tennessee Williams* (Macmillan Modern Dramatists), Petersen-Macmillan Verlag, Hamburg, 1987
> Follows the standard pattern of modern scholarship: a short biography followed by summaries of the plays

Signi Falk, *Tennessee Williams*, Twayne Publishers, 1961
> A discussion of Tennessee Williams' plays, with too much emphasis on summaries of the plots

Philip C. Kolin (ed.), *Confronting Tennessee' Williams's A Streetcar Named Desire* (Contributions in Drama and Theatre Studies, No. 50), Greenwood Press, Westport, Connecticut, 1993
> Academic contributions of varying value

Richard F. Leavitt (ed.), *The World of Tennessee Williams*, W. H. Allen, London, 1978
    A lot of illustrations, some interesting; very little text

Matthew C. Roudané (ed.), *The Cambridge Companion to Tennessee Williams* (Cambridge Companions to Literature), CUP, 1997
    Academic contributions by several scholars

Nancy M. Tischler, *Student Companion to Tennessee Williams* (Student Companions to Classic Writers), Greenwood Press, Westport, Connecticut, 2000
    Short biography followed by a discussion of the plays

**authorial voice** the author, as distinct from the characters he/she has created, speaking directly to the reader

**closet drama** a play written to be read, not acted on the stage

**coda** in music a concluding passage which provides a satisfying ending. It is now also used of a literary work

*coup de théâtre* (French) a sudden startling turn of events in a play

**deus ex machina** (Latin) originally an actor playing a god brought on the stage by a mechanical device. Used to describe a contrived and unconvincing twist in a plot, as a way out of a difficulty

**epigraph** quotation placed at the beginning of a poem, novel or play, hinting at its meaning

**Expressionist** presenting a distorted, exaggerated form of reality. The Expressionist movement started in Germany in the early twentieth century in visual arts, and exercised a considerable influence on drama and film as well as on literature

**figurative language** language enriched by figures of speech such as metaphor

**genre** distinctive type of literature

**hubris** (Greek) the overweening pride that is the cause of the downfall of a tragic hero

**leitmotiv** (German) recurring main theme (a borrowing from musical terminology)

**melodrama** play with a sensational plot, violent, often bloodthirsty incident, and with over-simple characterisation of heroes and villains

**pathos** quality which evokes strong feelings of pity and sorrow. This quality can of course be tinged with mawkish sentimentality, as in some of Dickens' work.

**succès de scandale** (French) literary work which owes its success partly or largely to its scandalous content, or to a scandal linked to its first appearance

**symbolism** the use of words to represent something else. The symbolist movement in nineteenth-century literature believed in hidden meanings underlying reality

*tableau vivant* a living picture, a group of silent motionless actors representing a dramatic event

**trope** any figure of speech in which a word is used to represent something else (a metaphor or a simile is a trope)

**unities** the rules demanding unity of time, place and action in a play. These rules came to be ascribed to the Greek critic and philosopher Aristotle, and from the sixteenth to the nineteenth century were regarded by literary theorists as imperative for the construction of a drama

# AUTHOR OF THESE NOTES

Hana Sambrook was educated at the Charles University in Prague and at the University of Edinburgh. She worked for some years as an editor in Scottish educational publishing, and was later on the staff of the Edinburgh University Library. Now a freelance editor in London, she is the author of several York Notes.

## General editors

Martin Gray, former Head of the Department of English Studies at the University of Stirling, and of Literary Studies at the University of Luton

Professor A. N. Jeffares, Emeritus Professor of English, University of Stirling

Maya Angelou
*I Know Why the Caged Bird Sings*

Jane Austen
*Pride and Prejudice*

Alan Ayckbourn
*Absent Friends*

Elizabeth Barrett Browning
*Selected Poems*

Robert Bolt
*A Man for All Seasons*

Harold Brighouse
*Hobson's Choice*

Charlotte Brontë
*Jane Eyre*

Emily Brontë
*Wuthering Heights*

Shelagh Delaney
*A Taste of Honey*

Charles Dickens
*David Copperfield*
*Great Expectations*
*Hard Times*
*Oliver Twist*

Roddy Doyle
*Paddy Clarke Ha Ha Ha*

George Eliot
*Silas Marner*
*The Mill on the Floss*

Anne Frank
*The Diary of a Young Girl*

William Golding
*Lord of the Flies*

Oliver Goldsmith
*She Stoops to Conquer*

Willis Hall
*The Long and the Short and the Tall*

Thomas Hardy
*Far from the Madding Crowd*
*The Mayor of Casterbridge*
*Tess of the d'Urbervilles*
*The Withered Arm and other Wessex Tales*

L.P. Hartley
*The Go-Between*

Seamus Heaney
*Selected Poems*

Susan Hill
*I'm the King of the Castle*

Barry Hines
*A Kestrel for a Knave*

Louise Lawrence
*Children of the Dust*

Harper Lee
*To Kill a Mockingbird*

Laurie Lee
*Cider with Rosie*

Arthur Miller
*The Crucible*
*A View from the Bridge*

Robert O'Brien
*Z for Zachariah*

Frank O'Connor
*My Oedipus Complex and Other Stories*

George Orwell
*Animal Farm*

J.B. Priestley
*An Inspector Calls*
*When We Are Married*

Willy Russell
*Educating Rita*
*Our Day Out*

J.D. Salinger
*The Catcher in the Rye*

William Shakespeare
*Henry IV Part I*
*Henry V*
*Julius Caesar*
*Macbeth*
*The Merchant of Venice*
*A Midsummer Night's Dream*
*Much Ado About Nothing*

*Romeo and Juliet*
*The Tempest*
*Twelfth Night*

George Bernard Shaw
*Pygmalion*

Mary Shelley
*Frankenstein*

R.C. Sherriff
*Journey's End*

Rukshana Smith
*Salt on the snow*

John Steinbeck
*Of Mice and Men*

Robert Louis Stevenson
*Dr Jekyll and Mr Hyde*

Jonathan Swift
*Gulliver's Travels*

Robert Swindells
*Daz 4 Zoe*

Mildred D. Taylor
*Roll of Thunder, Hear My Cry*

Mark Twain
*Huckleberry Finn*

James Watson
*Talking in Whispers*

Edith Wharton
*Ethan Frome*

William Wordsworth
*Selected Poems*

*A Choice of Poets*

*Mystery Stories of the Nineteenth Century including The Signalman*

*Nineteenth Century Short Stories*

*Poetry of the First World War*

*Six Women Poets*

For the AQA Anthology:

*Duffy and Armitage & Pre-1914 Poetry*

*Heaney and Clarke & Pre-1914 Poetry*

*Poems from Different Cultures*

Margaret Atwood
*Cat's Eye*
*The Handmaid's Tale*

Jane Austen
*Emma*
*Mansfield Park*
*Persuasion*
*Pride and Prejudice*
*Sense and Sensibility*

Alan Bennett
*Talking Heads*

William Blake
*Songs of Innocence and of Experience*

Charlotte Brontë
*Jane Eyre*
*Villette*

Emily Brontë
*Wuthering Heights*

Angela Carter
*Nights at the Circus*

Geoffrey Chaucer
*The Franklin's Prologue and Tale*
*The Merchant's Prologue and Tale*
*The Miller's Prologue and Tale*
*The Prologue to the Canterbury Tales*
*The Wife of Bath's Prologue and Tale*

Samuel Coleridge
*Selected Poems*

Joseph Conrad
*Heart of Darkness*

Daniel Defoe
*Moll Flanders*

Charles Dickens
*Bleak House*
*Great Expectations*
*Hard Times*

Emily Dickinson
*Selected Poems*

John Donne
*Selected Poems*

Carol Ann Duffy
*Selected Poems*

George Eliot
*Middlemarch*
*The Mill on the Floss*

T.S. Eliot
*Selected Poems*
*The Waste Land*

F. Scott Fitzgerald
*The Great Gatsby*

E.M. Forster
*A Passage to India*

Brian Friel
*Translations*

Thomas Hardy
*Jude the Obscure*
*The Mayor of Casterbridge*
*The Return of the Native*
*Selected Poems*
*Tess of the d'Urbervilles*

Seamus Heaney
*Selected Poems from 'Opened Ground'*

Nathaniel Hawthorne
*The Scarlet Letter*

Homer
*The Iliad*
*The Odyssey*

Aldous Huxley
*Brave New World*

Kazuo Ishiguro
*The Remains of the Day*

Ben Jonson
*The Alchemist*

James Joyce
*Dubliners*

John Keats
*Selected Poems*

Philip Larkin
*The Whitsun Weddings and Selected Poems*

Christopher Marlowe
*Doctor Faustus*
*Edward II*

Arthur Miller
*Death of a Salesman*

John Milton
*Paradise Lost Books I & II*

Toni Morrison
*Beloved*

George Orwell
*Nineteen Eighty-Four*

Sylvia Plath
*Selected Poems*

Alexander Pope
*Rape of the Lock & Selected Poems*

William Shakespeare
*Antony and Cleopatra*
*As You Like It*
*Hamlet*
*Henry IV Part I*
*King Lear*
*Macbeth*
*Measure for Measure*
*The Merchant of Venice*
*A Midsummer Night's Dream*
*Much Ado About Nothing*
*Othello*
*Richard II*
*Richard III*
*Romeo and Juliet*
*The Taming of the Shrew*
*The Tempest*
*Twelfth Night*
*The Winter's Tale*

George Bernard Shaw
*Saint Joan*

Mary Shelley
*Frankenstein*

Jonathan Swift
*Gulliver's Travels and A Modest Proposal*

Alfred Tennyson
*Selected Poems*

Virgil
*The Aeneid*

Alice Walker
*The Color Purple*

Oscar Wilde
*The Importance of Being Earnest*

Tennessee Williams
*A Streetcar Named Desire*
*The Glass Menagerie*

Jeanette Winterson
*Oranges Are Not the Only Fruit*

John Webster
*The Duchess of Malfi*

Virginia Woolf
*To the Lighthouse*

William Wordsworth
*The Prelude and Selected Poems*

W.B. Yeats
*Selected Poems*

*Metaphysical Poets*